Women Empowerment and Development

Women Empowerment and Development

Readings from Asia

Edited by

SAMEERA MAITI

RAWAT PUBLICATIONS

Jaipur • New Delhi • Bangalore • Guwahati • Kolkata

ISBN 978-81-316-0786-2

Published by
Prem Rawat for **Rawat Publications**
Satyam Apts, Sector 3, Jawahar Nagar, Jaipur 302 004 (India)
Phone: 0141 265 1748 / 7006 Fax: 0141 265 1748
E-mail: info@rawatbooks.com
Website: www.rawatbooks.com

New Delhi Office
4858/24, Ansari Road, Daryaganj, New Delhi 110 002
Phone: 011 2326 3290

Also at *Bangalore, Guwahati* and *Kolkata*

Typeset by Rawat Computers, Jaipur
Printed at Chaman Enterprises, New Delhi

Contents

Foreword

The present volume documents the various developments that have taken place in the field of gender equity, affirmative legislations for women's empowerment, the conceptual graduation from 'women in development' to 'women and development' to 'gender and development', etc. The volume also brings to the fore the fact that understanding of women's issues is a complex matter that needs multi-disciplinary approach.

No one perhaps disagrees with the general tonality of the book. We all agree that women need empowerment and development. But is that enough to attain gender equity? Are we not missing out on some important dimensions of gender in our, what I would like to call 'missionary' approach to women's development? In this foreword to a book on women's empowerment edited by a woman I consider it important to draw the attention of the readers of this book to some of those missing dimensions of gender.

One such dimension is the assumption that women are powerless, voiceless, and 'space'-less. But is it correct to believe that power, voice and space are the monopoly of men, both in time and space? What appears to be sadly missing here is the acceptance of the fact that there are men, as well as women in our society, who need empowerment because a vast majority of them are illiterate, unemployed, poor, exploited and marginalized. It is certainly true, at least in developing countries, that larger percentage of women than men are illiterate, unemployed and poor, but that does not mean that men do not need empowerment. Equality of opportunity, which in any way cannot be guaranteed in absolute sense anywhere in the world, actually becomes a hoax call for women who have lesser opportunity, but a big chunk of men belonging to Scheduled Castes, for instance, are not equal with other high caste men and hence need empowerment to come at par with high caste men.

Shifting of attention from the equation between men and women to equations within men and within women is often seen as a misogynist ploy of men to deflect attention from the incapacities women suffer from. I, as a man, am not sure if this is indeed so, as feminists would like us to believe. Does talking about lack of equity within each gender have no merit even academically speaking? Are all men, or for that matter all women, equal? The answer is certainly no, nor is that ever possible. Inequality is built in our social system, and new opportunities have further entrenched it rather than brought a more egalitarian society. They have actually widened the spectrum of inequality rather than narrowed it down. Discriminatory practices towards women are perhaps more institutionalized among the higher classes/castes members, as they are more feudal in their outlook and their women are more marginalized (under the guise of being 'protected' or 'taken care of' etc.), than for instance among the lower classes/castes where women are often the main bread-earners. It is also observed that women in paddy-growing areas are less subjected to patriarchal exploitations than those in wheat-growing areas, due perhaps to the fact that women have greater economic role to play in the former than in the latter.

One could well ignore if intra-men and intra-women inequalities could be considered as less important than inequalities between men and women. One could certainly ignore such inequalities if men and women lived separately and not as members of same families, clans, castes, communities, societies and so on. Not only do men prevent women from doing many jobs but women also prevent men from doing many jobs. While women may not be able to physically prevent men from doing what men want to do they can use their 'soft power' to persuade men not to do what they do not like their men to do.

We all know that men are not raped, molested or groped but they too can be vulnerable to physical and sexual abuse when they are young and the same may continue if they are poor. However it is generally young girls and women who have to experience all this in the hands of men in bus, train, office, etc. Men are rarely stripped naked and paraded in the village chowks or city lanes, but women are often subjected to such indignity. It is not surprising that while men can be witch doctors only women can be 'witches'!

It is generally admitted that both men and women are physically capable of doing the same things but are culturally trained to do different kinds of things. Should we reduce this fact to a sign of control and domination by men over women? Does doing different kinds of jobs by men and women indicate superiority of men to women? Are we not looking at the cultural division of labour in our societies from a western, binary perspective? Must both men and women do the same jobs in order to achieve gender equity? Can men and women not do different things and yet be equal? I strongly suspect that opening every kind of job for both men and women to compete may lead to further marginalization and exploitation of women. I think it is necessary to abandon the much harped and hyped perspective of men and women as different species and embrace the eastern perspective that sees an overlap between them. This overlap has always existed and will be visible if intra-men and intra-women differences in access, power, opportunity, status, etc. are recognized.

I have often wondered why atrocities and often inhuman crimes continue to be committed against women in spite of numerous laws protecting them. One of the reasons, in my humble opinion, is the poverty of our approach to women, seeing them as we do as a separate category from men, as if they are a different species altogether. Remember the adage 'Men are from Mars and Women from Venus!' I personally think that we have far too long kept men and women apart by erecting a false wall of gender between them. Unless we see them in symbiotic relationship our noble goal of empowering women will continue to evade us. Let us admit that women also bask in the glory of patriarchy when the situation is favourable for them. Let us not look at every man through feminist lens and let us not certify every woman to be weak and harmless. Modern warfare is after all not about muscles, but about technology and brains.

If you disagree with me you should read this book. If you agree you should still read it.

Prof. T.B. Subba
Vice-Chancellor, Sikkim University
Gangtok

Preface

This volume is a curated and edited selection of papers accepted for presentation at my convened panel on "Women's Empowerment, Development and Quality of Life" at the Inter Congress 2014 of the International Union of Anthropological and Ethnological Sciences (IUAES), the largest world forum of anthropologists and ethnologists, held at Chiba City, Japan from 15-18 May, 2014. The panel aimed at relating the three important concepts of empowerment, development and quality of life in the context of women, who are recognised universally as a disadvantaged group despite endeavours at international, national and local levels to provide them an equal position with men. I would like to thank the authors of the papers in this volume for their contributions, and the Organizing Committee of IUAES 2014 for acceptance of my proposed panel.

Professor T.B. Subba, Vice-Chancellor of Sikkim University, a distinguished anthropologist and expert on North Eastern issues and marginalized peoples, has been gracious enough to write a foreword to this book. Special thanks are due to him for his contribution, kind words of encouragement and sustained mentorship.

I appreciate the efforts by Pranit Rawat, our publisher, in bringing this book to fruition. Thanks are due to Dr Riddhi Srivastava, Lecturer National P.G. College who helped out with the final proof. I would also like to thank my family for their encouragement and support when this volume was being put together.

Gangtok **Sameera Maiti**

1

Women's Development and Empowerment

An Introduction

SAMEERA MAITI

The principles of humanity, equality and justice let us assume that every person is entitled to enjoy and improve their existing quality of life using resources of betterment available in their respective societies. But the fact remains that such uniformity of opportunity does not exist and that is why one speaks of 'empowering' the weaker sections and developing special policies and programmes to bring them at an equal footing with those in power. Empowerment in simple terms means to attempt to make a person (who till now has been subjugated, dominated or depressed) 'powerful' enough to take their own decisions and lead a life of equality and respect. Further, 'in seeking "development" or "progress" we seek happiness and better quality of life' (Ghosh 1992: 35). Thus, the three concepts, viz. development, empowerment and quality of life are closely interrelated. Over the past few decades, words such as 'women's development', 'women's empowerment' and 'improved quality of life for women' have greatly been used at an international level by academicians, development agencies, non-governmental organizations, civil societies as well as by the administration/government of all countries while discussing issues related to gender equality and sustainable development.

Women's status, especially in the developing countries, is intimately affected by complex social conditions such as gender inequality, poverty, lack of education, child mortality, maternal ill-health, HIV/AIDS, non-participation in public forums, all of which result in a poor quality of life. This further restricts their participation in the development process. It is well known that women's active participation in the development process is closely related to the comprehensive socio-economic development of any society and any strategy which neglects the need for enhancing the role of women cannot lead to comprehensive development. The issue of women's development is of great importance since the status of half of this world's population has been lagging behind in all major areas where power is wielded. It is a universally accepted fact that although women contribute equally and sometimes even more than men, in the society's socio-economic activities their role and contributions are hardly ever recognized or acknowledged and they are almost never involved in political and economic decision-making.

According to a United Nations Development Programme report (2011) 'Despite progress in recent years, women and girls account for six out of 10 of the world's poorest and two thirds of the world's illiterate people. Only 19 per cent of the world's parliamentarians are women and one third of all women are subjected to violence whether in times of armed conflict or behind closed doors at home'. The report also mentions that although women constitute half the world's population, they 'perform 66 per cent of the world's work, produce 50 per cent of the food, but earn only 10 per cent of the income and own only one per cent of the property.' This neglect leads to their non-involvement in all major decision-making due to which they have no power whatsoever and continue to remain marginalized. Their access to resources is limited as is their access to health-care, quality education and various other factors that would ensure a good quality of life and overall well-being.

In the context of most Asian women too it has been acknowledged and proved time and again in various studies that although they contribute more than their male counterparts by putting in more labour in performing most, if not all, of the household chores and agricultural work, they never get the credit for the same. This lack of acknowledgement and appreciation for their efforts no doubt has a direct effect on their self-image, self-worth and ultimate well-being. In most cases, however, women continue to suffer due to their unawareness regarding the concept of 'equality of the sexes' and being socialized from their very birth about the superiority of men, as a result of living in a patriarchal system. Under the circumstance, the first step towards empowering them is making them aware and conscious of their rights and capabilities.

Today, concerted efforts are being made at every level globally to involve women in the process of development. The governments of almost all countries, including India, through various developmental and welfare schemes are trying to empower women and to increase their active and formal involvement in every sphere of life and thereby to improve their overall status. However, a great gap still exists between policies and practice, as is evident from several of the papers included in the current volume. Lack of gender equality and equity is all pervasive – whether it be in China's megacities or its rural countryside; inequalities exist in societies as diverse as those of Himalayan ascetics to the tribal forests and badlands in Central India and Odisha, from the fertile plains of the Punjab to materially developed Japan.

During the initial stages, women's development worldwide was merely considered a part of the larger process of modernization which, it was assumed, would lead to the overall development of all irrespective of class, caste, race or gender. Rahman (1999: 14) rightly states that the modernization paradigm did not consider women separately as a group since it was assumed that a modern secular society would automatically improve women's situation by freeing women from the constraint of traditional culture.

The assumptions of the modernization theory were criticized by Boserup (1970) who showed how the needs of women had been overlooked and argued for women's integration as equal partners with men in the development process. Boserup's work led to a new approach known as Women in Development (WID) which highlighted the role and importance of women in development. WID believed that women could be empowered within the capitalist development by incorporating them in the production process whereby they would have access to an expanding monetary economy (Rahman 1999). WID stressed that women be provided access to developmental resources and newer employment opportunities and their role in production be recognized and given due importance (Tinker 1990). Thus, WID deals with women's role, status and decision-making powers in relation to economic activities and highlighted the need to integrate women as active agents in the development process if effective and efficient development was to be achieved (Reeves and Baden 2000).

The Women and Development (WAD) approach came up in the late 70s as an alternative that criticized the WID approach for ignoring the capitalist nature of the developmental process with its inherent socio-cultural and gendered inequalities. WAD brought forward the fact that socio-cultural inequalities, patriarchy and capitalism, all had a restraining and limiting effect on the options available for women's development and empowerment. Thus, as Connelly et al. (2000) noted, WAD stresses upon the distinctiveness of women's knowledge, women's work, and women's goals and responsibilities.

The latest interdisciplinary approach of Gender and Development (GAD), which emerged in the 1980s, deals with the entire question of imbalance of power between the genders and is a more comprehensive approach encapsulating all fields of gendered discrimination. This approach includes aspects of both WID and WAD while emphasizing that changes in women's condition can be achieved by overcoming traditional gendered stereotyping, ideologies and inequalities. GAD is based on the basic premise that women in every society represent an oppressed, discriminated, unequal and disadvantaged social category who need to be empowered if one is to achieve sustainable development. Thus, it favours the elimination of every kind of social, customary or legal constraint that hampers women's mobility and equal participation in the overall development process. It argues that a women friendly environment and women sensitive socio-economic policies combined with women's self-empowerment through their capacity building and mobilization in an organized manner will lead to an improved overall status and quality of life for women. Thus, GAD challenges the existing gender roles and power relations while aiming to meet both women's practical gender needs and more strategic gender needs (Reeves and Baden 2000). In short, it does not merely focus on women but on the relations between men and women. It sees gendered relations as the key determinants of women's status and position in society rather than as reflections of the natural order – a social construction of gender which can be changed if desired (Connelly et al. 2000).

Women's movements and feminist thinkers, on the other hand, have in fact even questioned all the existing models of development, which provide parameters within which one is forced to think and act. They advocate structural and cultural transformation of the society, which would help create a more egalitarian relationship between men and women and for this, empowerment of women is the most essential condition.

'Empowerment' became a buzzword since the 1990s when the development approach began to be modified by a newer 'welfare' approach that viewed women as beneficiaries of various services and concessions. The new approach, while emphasizing the importance of the GAD approach, aimed at empowering women by making them independent and active players in all aspects of their lives.

Empowerment, as Beteille (1999: 590) states, 'may be invoked in virtually any context' and aims at bringing about a change in the general and power relations since it 'seeks to change society through a rearrangement of power' (ibid.: 591). Further, empowerment is about 'ordinary, common people rather than politicians, experts and other socially or culturally advantaged persons' (ibid.: 590). It is a means to overcome disabilities through a wide range of strategies that alter the positions that have been in existence since long. Empowerment, however, can only occasionally be achieved through individual efforts. In most cases the process involves an organized attempt to attain power with the help of various organizations (women's organizations in this case) and other agencies which can perform the task of pressurizing the government on various issues of concern. Through their demands these organizations persuade and at times force governments to frame women friendly or women specific programmes and policies aiming at their overall development.

It is such pressures that further lead to attention being paid to women as a disadvantaged social group on an international level wherein efforts for their development and empowerment are made. While development/welfare are spoken of and measured in terms of economic participation, literacy level, health care, access to resources and all kinds of material advancement, empowerment includes much more than this. Empowerment requires an awareness and inclination for self-betterment on part of women themselves, i.e. a change in their attitude with awareness towards their own capabilities and potentialities is necessary. Women's empowerment also requires a fundamental and dynamic change in perception of women in society; expectations from them; and a systematic and sympathetic understanding of their problems and needs. Thus, empowerment is an essential tool to bring about a change in the status and position held by women in every society, be it a developing or developed one.

Even in Japan, which is considered to be the most developed among the Asian nations, equality among the sexes has not been achieved. Fujikake in her paper (Chapter 2) points out this very fact when she brings out the discrepancy that exists in merely asserting, by the Japanese government that 'gender mainstreaming has been accomplished' and the actual ground realities. Through her paper she highlights that the government is to a great extent being influenced by statements such as the above and arguments by the pro-backlash people to cut back on an aid for people (women, in this case) who are structurally relegated to subordinate roles in society and need assistance. She brings forward the need to redefine GAD in such a way that it is helpful to highlight gender issues on site and facilitate concrete discussions for practical assistance which will help in gender mainstreaming.

Carr, Chen and Jhabvala (1997: 1) rightly state that a major cause of poverty in South Asia is the 'entrenched traditional structure'. Compounding this, is the ensuing powerlessness which further aggravates feelings of inadequacy. Moreover, when victims of poverty happen to be women, their situation is further complicated by the instituted structural inequalities between the sexes which are inherent in every community, in addition to the constraints of religion, rules of patrilineal descent and the absence of workable rules of inheritance. Clear evidence in this direction is presented by Wang and Zhang (Chapter 3) in the context of China's 'gendered membership' where the legal land rights of the *Nong Jia Nv* ('left over women', i.e. unmarried, widowed, divorced or married but living in their village of birth) are usurped leaving them in abject poverty to fend for themselves. Legal membership rights here would entail access to contractible land, housing land and other collective services such as opportunities for rural industrial employment. While analysing the situation from the feminist, historical and institutional perspectives, the authors show how Chinese rural society is still under a very strict patriarchal structure. Virilocal marriage pattern and a patrilineal system of contracted land distribution and inheritance form an institutionalized barrier for rural women's marriage or employment-oriented migration thereby opening the space for villages' self-governance and expropriation of a woman's legal rights. In practice, many village committees have adopted a criterion that make women's 'membership' conditional to their marriage to local men, thereby perpetuating men's control of collective and household wealth. The authors bring out that although gender inequalities in civil, political, economic and social entitlements have widened after the land expropriation and stock cooperative reform of China since 1990s, scholars rarely address the issue of gender stratification and inequalities while women continue to suffer due to this silence.

The above case proves beyond doubt that one of the grossly neglected dimensions of gender equality is the 'effective control of the use of property – public as well as private' (Loutfi 2002: 4). Gender discrimination in land ownership and other productive assets has a direct bearing on women's status and places them in disadvantaged situation both in terms of securing a place to live and for earning their livelihood. One of the reasons for this is gender unequal laws/policies besides the prevailing socio-cultural value system, as already stated before. Post 1990, there has been a considerable progress in making formal laws pertaining to landed property more gender equitable. Many developing countries have enacted laws, framed policies and amended constitutions to guarantee rights of women on an equitable basis. In order to empower women economically, some states in India have also initiated a scheme of providing reduction in the stamp duty levied while purchasing property, if the same is registered in a woman's name. Arora and Singh, in Chapter 4, discuss these concessions, in the context of the state of Uttar Pradesh, as being based on the basic premise that ownership of productive resources by women would make them socially and economically secure, reduce the chances of domestic violence and enable their overall empowerment. In their study, the authors found that, although the scheme had a positive effect in the direction of enabling women's control over property, in ten per cent cases the women were immediately made to give the power of attorney to a male member thus stripping them of any control whatsoever over the property that was registered in their name to avail tax concessions. Despite this, it remains a fact that incentives such as the one being discussed can provide economic security and confidence to women while increasing their level of acceptance/respect in the family and increasing their role in decision-making.

Over the years, as a result of the combined efforts of industrialization, urbanization, and feminist movements, women have been drawn into the labour force, bringing them out of the four walls of the house where they had been confined to for ages. Globalization and liberalization further have had a positive effect on the patterns of employment available for women. This leads to a greater access over resources, a better control over one's life and ultimately an improved quality of life. An example of this can be seen in Gupta and Mehta's paper (Chapter 5) where, through narratives collected from the field, the authors show how women in rural Punjab use their traditional hand embroidery skills to create a variety of much demanded marketable products. The authors found that in addition to empowerment, involvement in such economically viable activities help women gain self-confidence and add value to their status in the household, community and village. It also helped improve women's level of confidence to take decisions independently and spend the money earned to improve their own and their family's quality of life.

According to Coger and Kanungo (1998: 474), 'empowered people believe that they are competent and valued, that their jobs have meaning and impact and that they have opportunities to use their talent'. Such opportunities and resultant positive changes, however, are not available to all women equally and are restricted to mainly urban women and a few selected groups/clusters of women in rural areas as is brought out by Xiang and Isbister (Chapter 6) in their research. They argue that in the context of urbanization, land loss, and land use regulations for the rural area in China, serving in *Nongjiale*, a form of rural tourism as an alternative livelihood strategy has reshaped the rural women's life and enhanced their subjective well-being to a great extent. However, not all women even from the same village can benefit equally, since to start a *Nongjiale* business, one needs some start up funds/seed money. The result has been that families with considerable savings have seized the opportunity, while the economically constrained women were deprived of even a chance to participate. Although well intended, there is no doubt that such a scheme would ultimately lead to a further polarization of the rich and the poor in the villages rather than serve the purpose of equitable or sustainable development of all. The case in discussion clearly proves that before implementing any scheme for women's development or empowerment, the existing conditions of the intended beneficiaries and their capability to participate/benefit from the scheme should be evaluated and taken into consideration. This is essential so that women from every socio-economic strata get an equal opportunity to participate and benefit from the scheme.

One means of achieving justice is affirmative action, which is 'an extension of the notion of equality of opportunity and non-discrimination' (Aeberhard year cf. Loutfi 2002: 4). In an attempt to redress the current situation of gender imbalance and discrimination existing in the country, the Government of India established the National Commission on Women by an Act of Parliament in 1990 to safeguard the rights and legal entitlements of women, in addition to various measures for their upliftment and empowerment. Debnath (Chapter 7), through examples drawn from two case studies in the states of Madhya Pradesh and Chhattisgarh, shows that in community mobilization local NGOs (non-governmental organizations) and community-based organizations have taken up a significant role. It has been found that formation of Self-Help Groups (SHGs) of tribal women is the best organizational process to generate livelihood as well as provide equity and sustainability. The author feels that, following the National Forest Policy of 1988 and 1990 on Joint Forest Management, tribal women have been considered as key stakeholders in Participatory Forest Management and they are being involved while taking decisions relating to natural resources management and community development. Despite this, a wide gap exists between the goals enunciated in various legislations, polices, plans, programmes and related mechanisms for women's empowerment on one hand and the situational reality of the conditions and status of women in India on the other. This is evident from Satpathy's paper (Chapter 8) which, drawing upon the case of the tribal women of the Indian state of Odisha, shows that although various policies and programmes have been adopted by the government and NGOs for promoting livelihood access to women, these have not been successful to a significant extent mainly due their ignorance, illiteracy and lack of exposure to the outside world. Her study reveals that simple and low input intensive technologies of a small scale are quickly accepted by tribal women since these would have compatibility with the tribal culture. It also proves that, there is a strong correlation between the acceptance of development programmes and the kind of technology being used to implement these programmes and also reiterates the need to alter the development approach in order to achieve desired result. Hence, a parental top-down (trickle-down) approach of development does not generally suffice. For successful development and empowerment the bottom-up participatory development would certainly be the best suited and more prone to succeed.

Authority and leadership is another area where women have traditionally been losing out. Politics has largely remained a male domain throughout the world with women rarely wielding any authority at all. Further, despite myths about women in the Amazon or various matrilineal societies, women are nowhere in the world found to be rulers. In every society of the world, women are considered a degree inferior/lower to men because of which they generally have to depend on consent from men before taking any major decision and are therefore not allowed to hold positions of power and authority. It was probably keeping these facts in mind that the 73rd Amendment Act was passed in 1994 by the Indian Parliament mandating reservation of 33 per cent seats in all village, block and district levels elected bodies for women. To a certain extent, because of this Act, women today can be seen as leaders in the political arena at local levels. However, even twenty years after the Act's passage and despite all efforts to empower women through it, not much of actual 'empowerment' has been achieved. This is evident also from Bhawna's study among the Gond tribal women (Chapter 9) which reveals that although their level of political awareness and participation has increased as a result of reservation being given to women in the political field, they remain powerless due to their ignorance, illiteracy and poverty – all of which combine to act as pull back factors in the realization of actual empowerment. The author rightly concluded that it is the women themselves who have to strive hard to become actual possessors of power and in this effort they must work twice as hard as their male counterparts to be recognized and make their presence felt.

A similar scenario exists not only when talking of political power and authority. In fact any situation that entails some kind of hierarchy of position, authority and power always has women either at the lowest levels, or restricted from rising to the highest levels by the existence of a glass ceiling – conditions that act as a hurdle or obstruction in their upward movement. In fact, gender inequalities and discriminations' are so deeply ingrained in our psyche that even Buddhism, which is often promulgated as an egalitarian and gender-neutral religion by mainstream Buddhist scholars, has not remained unaffected by this. Sachdeva and Bothe in their paper (Chapter 10) show, through empirical narratives, the strong patriarchal connotations and gender hierarchies that exist in everyday contemporary monastic practices where annies have a much tougher regime and rules to follow, compared to monks while being relegated to perform mundane chores of the ritual performances, while monks, even young ones, are allowed to chant the religious texts. Moving up the rank too is nearly impossible for an annie. An example is that while to become a *Galong* a monk needs to follow two hundred and fifty (250) vows, for getting initiated to the equivalent rank of a *Galongma* there are three hundred and sixty four (364) vows to be followed by the annie.

According to Coger and Kanungo (1998: 474) 'from the standpoint of assumption that powerlessness gives rise to low self-efficiency ... (empowerment is) a process of identifying and removing the conditions which cause powerlessness while increasing feelings of self-efficacy'. The feeling of powerlessness among women, and especially women who are mothers can have adverse intergenerational impact. A study on mothers of children with learning disabilities, by Chowdhary (Chapter 11), revealed that a majority of them had very little knowledge regarding cause, treatment, and remedies of their child's disability because of which they not only suffered from low self-esteem but also started withdrawing from active social life. The author, calls for empowerment of these mothers, since they are the primary care takers of the children, while proposing that this lack of empowerment leads to poorer health outcomes for children with disabilities and special needs.

Moser (1993), rightly states that world over women experience oppression and discrimination in a variety of ways depending on their race, class, culture, colonial history and even position in the international economic order. In most of Asia, it is well accepted that the status of women is much lower than that of men, and this is clearly depicted in almost all the papers included in this volume. Most Asian countries are quite populous and exhibit several regional, developmental and cultural variations and disparities within their own national boundaries that add to the vulnerability of women and make the situation here more complex. Factors such as lack of or limited access to the resources of development, lesser economically viable skills, lower earnings, low literacy levels, malnutrition, poor standards of health, lack of freedom and opportunities, lack of autonomy, lesser or no role in decision-making, greater exposure to domestic violence and sexual crimes are to a great extent both responsible for and an outcome of the inferior status of women.

The World Conference on Women (1995: 16) in Chapter III, no. 41 states that:

> The advancement of women and the achievement of equality between women and men are a matter of human rights and a condition for social justice and should not be seen in isolation as a women's issue. They are the only way to build a sustainable, just and developed society. Empowerment of women and equality between women and men are prerequisites for achieving political, social, economic, cultural and environmental security among all peoples.

Although the concept of men and women being considered as equals has now achieved global acceptance, and relating equality of the sexes to human rights has made women more visible in nearly every sphere of life, equality has not yet been achieved anywhere. Despite it being more than a century since equality among the sexes was first spoken about, the process of change, transformation and adjustment to bring about 'equality' is still said to be continuing. Gender stereotyping, that is so deeply ingrained in the social norms of patriarchy, adds to the persistence of inequality. This is the chief reason why we still need to speak of and make special efforts towards women's development and empowerment.

Given the existing circumstances, the key need is for the state's intervention to not only to formulate, but to actively implement and monitor positive policies and affirmative action programmes focused on women's development and empowerment. Furthermore, a greater involvement of women in framing policies and programmes that are meant for women's development and empowerment is called for. A woman's perspective and understanding of women's needs can help overcome several seemingly insignificant issues and problems that could later render the best formulated programmes ineffective.

Furthermore, active state policies can lead to changes on the ground only through proper implementation. Proper implementation can be achieved through the active and earnest involvement of the targeted women themselves, and for this involvement it is essential that the women are made aware of and support the concepts of equality and empowerment. Thus creating awareness towards and a desire for equality and empowerment too is essential. In addition, there is a need for soft empowerment and cultural transformation to bring about a change in the ingrained mindset that women are, in any way, lesser than men. Creating a gender sensitive environment where women are truly accepted as equal partners of men is a must. Once this aim is achieved, probably we will have no more need to speak of and strive for women's development and empowerment.

REFERENCES

Beteille, A. (1999) 'Empowerment', *Economic and Political Weekly*, 34 (10–11), 6–13 March.

Boserup, E. (1970) *Women's Role in Economic Development*. London: George Allen and Unwin.

Carr, M., M. Chen and R. Jhabvala (1997) *Speaking Out: Women's Empowerment in South Asia*. London: IT Publications.

Coger, J.A. and R.N. Kanungo (1998) 'The Empowerment Process: Integrating Theory and Practice', *Academy of Management Review*, 13 (3).

Connelly, M.P., T.M. Li, M. MacDonald and J.L. Parpart (2000) Feminism and Development: Theoretical Perspectives. In J.L. Parpart, M.P. Connelly and V.E. Barriteau (Eds), *Theoretical Perspectives on Gender and Development*. Ottawa: IDRC.

Ghosh, Sailendra Nath (1992) Development Strategy for a Better Quality of Life. In A. Datta and M.M. Agarwal (Eds), *The Quality of Life*. Shimla: IIAS.

Loutfi, M.F. (2002) Women, Gender and Work: An Overview. In M.F. Loutfi (Ed.), *Women, Gender and Work: What is Equality and How Do We Get There?* Jaipur: Rawat Publications and Geneva: International Labour Office.

Moser, C. (1993) *Gender, Planning and Development: Theory, Practice and Training*. London: Routledge.

Rahman, A. (1999) *Women and Micro Credit in Rural Bangladesh.* Boulder, CO: Westview Press.

Reeves, H. and S. Baden (2000) *Gender and Development: Concepts and Definitions* (Report No. 55). Brighton: IDS, University of Sussex. Retrieved on 25 September 2012 from http://www.bridge.ids.ac.uk/reports/re55.pdf

Tinker, L. (1990) *Persistent Inequalities: Women and World Development.* New York: Oxford University Press.

UNDP (2011) *Fast Facts: Gender Equality and UNDP.* New York: United Nations Development Programme.

WHO (1998) *WHO Quality of Life: User Manual.* Geneva: World Health Organisation.

World Conference on Women (1995) *Beijing Declaration and Platform for Action.* Beijing: The Fourth World Conference on Women. Retrieved on 12 June 2013 from http://www.un.org/womenwatch/daw/beijing/pdf/bdpfa%20e.pdf

2

'Gender and Development' Issues in Japan

The Reconstruction of Theory and Practice for Women's Empowerment

YOKO FUJIKAKE

If one were to question whether gender sensitive support activities have been sufficient with regards to the emergency aid and subsequent reconstruction aid in response to the Great East Japan Earthquake (11 March 2011), one must conclude that they have not been sensitive enough. In the 2011 Conference of the International Society for Gender Studies, a symposium with the theme '*Assistance and Gender*' was held in which several gender issues were brought to light (Fujikake 2012). In the special session, 'Disaster Reconstruction and New Development in International Cooperation' of the 22nd Fall Conference of the Japan Society for International Development, a prominent Japanese society focusing on international cooperation, held on 27 November 2011, no mention whatsoever of any gender issues were made. In the 'Earthquake and Disaster' Session of the 13th Spring Conference of the Same Society (1 June 2012), it was revealed that there were no gender sensitive support activities.

However, on 27 September 2013, more than one third of Prime Minister Shinzo Abe's speech to the United Nations General Assembly, expounded on the plan by Official Development Assistance (ODA) to spend in excess of three billion dollars in three years to deal with problems, such as the social progress of women and the protection of women's rights in conflict areas, under the slogan, 'Creation of a society where women can shine'.

The purpose of this paper is to verify the feasibility and obstacles of an open study pertaining to Women in/and Development (WID)/Gender and Development (GAD), initiated in the 1960s with much accumulated knowledge in several assistance fields; to review the development of GAD and the backlash movement in Japan to verify the effectiveness, feasibility and obstacles of the 'Creation of a society where women can shine' policy presented by the current government.

The outline of this paper is as follows: The first section is a general overview of the institutionalization of GAD and the academic issues confronting it; the next section reveals the backlash to gender policies in Japan and reviews criticisms to Japanese GAD policies in development fields. It is thought that the deepening of gender theory and the backlash movement has resulted in the creation of groups who distance themselves from gender, as well as making development practitioners hesitant to involve themselves in GAD. One explanation is that it is deemed 'not necessary to (specifically) discuss gender mainstreaming as it was previously accomplished'. The third section reveals that gender mainstreaming is never truly 'accomplished' with references to trainee comments from developing countries. Subsequently, the study distinguishing between GAD in the narrow sense and GAD in the broad sense needs an analytical framework to re-examine the aforementioned backlash and criticisms to GAD theory. The fourth section, based on the aforementioned study, discusses the results attributed to GAD up to the present and the difficulties and potential of GAD in the future. The Conclusion examines GAD as an open study and connects it to the Japanese Prime Minister's speech that 'women can shine in Japan'.

The Institutionalization of GAD and Confronting Issues

Institutionalized WID/GAD

There are numerous papers on the circumstances surrounding the emergence of WID and GAD as fields of study (Tinker 1990; Tanaka 1995; Ito 1995; Muramatsu 1997), therefore only a general overview related to its institutionalization is discussed here. The 'integration of women in development efforts' was clarified in the International Development Strategy adopted by the United Nations General Assembly (October 1970) and was approved as one of the pillars of the Second United Nations Development Decade. At the same time, due to the adoption of the Percy Amendment in the United States, programmes to 'encourage and promote the integration of women' were facilitated in development assistance policies and the Office for WID was created within the United States Agency for International Development (USAID). WID was boosted by the International Women's Year and the United Nations Decade for Women which influenced United Nations' policies, and later expanded to various United Nations' organizations, the World Bank and the IMF. In this process, WID itself morphed into 'institutionalized WID'. Since 1983, the Organization for Economic Co-operation and Development/Development Assistance Committee (OECD/DAC) has proposed that every nation reflects WID's point of view in their development cooperation.

In February 1990, the Japan International Cooperation Agency (JICA) established the 'Development and Women' study group, which in February 1991 presented proposals on basic measures to integrate WID's point of view into projects. It was in that time period when 'institutionalized WID/GAD' was established in Japan. Take for example the case of the Japan Overseas Cooperation Volunteers (JOCV), a volunteer programme of JICA. Since the early 1990s, occupational categories and requirements for which only men had been recruited were abandoned when the 'regardless of sex' provision was introduced; gender-neutral occupational categories where women play an active role have increased. As JICA followed the global tendency to shift priorities in the area of social development, recruitment for occupational categories/areas relating to agriculture and civil engineering, mainly the domain of men, has decreased; recruitment in occupational categories/areas relating to education and health, mainly the domain of women or gender-neutral, has increased. The change in recruitment practices coincides with the period that JICA began gender mainstreaming activities and WID activities (Fujikake 2011b). The Equal Employment Opportunity Law implemented in 1985, is considered one of the reasons for the increased participation of women in JOCV.

With regard to the policies in Japan, legislation promoting gender-equality was adopted in one local government after another due to the approval of the Basic Act for a Gender-Equal Society in June 1999. Terms such as 'gender sensitive approach', 'free from gender restraints' and 'gender-equal society'[1] began to be included in compulsory educational textbooks of Civics and Technology and Home Economics in junior high schools. Penetration of gender concepts throughout the country and penetration of WID/GAD concepts in JICA occurred during the same time period.

Issues Confronting GAD: What is Gender Mainstreaming?

The adoption of gender sensitive approach in international cooperation projects is expressed as 'gender mainstreaming'. The term gender mainstreaming was adopted for the first time in the 'Beijing Platform for Actions' by the Fourth World Conference on Women (FWCW or Beijing Conference) in 1995.[2] Gender mainstreaming is not a goal but measures to promote gender equality. However, the following three issues emerged in step with recognition of the need to incorporate GAD in development policies and practice, in other words, GAD's institutionalization:

1. Because of the trend toward gender mainstreaming, interventions for poor women with its interdisciplinary characteristics are considered to be everybody's responsibility, however the result is that nobody takes any responsibility (Chant 2007). Gender issues in Japanese assistance policies are thought to have suffered the same fate.
2. As a result of the institutionalization of GAD, the concept has become a mere shell and was depoliticized (Cornwall, Harrison and Whitehead 2004; Fujikake 2011b). The basis of GAD began from ideas, such as from Development Alternatives with Women for a New Era (DAWN), however with the institutionalization of GAD, its concepts are trivialized or depoliticized with the creation of a strategic accord (ibid.). The GAD theory adopts much of the theoretical framework upon which the Feminism theory relies, however depoliticization forces GAD not to question

authority, which results in GAD being implemented with many contradictions.

3. There is a gap between the universal framework which GAD's analytical theory encompasses and the local context of the third world.

Issues 1 and 2 are connected to difficulties in gender mainstreaming of development policies at the global/national level, and issue 3 is related to difficulties in GAD practice at the local level (ibid.). The author points to the classical debate of Mohanty's criticism (1986), whereby GAD has used 'the Western eyes' as the principle target of its theories and practice and designated others as 'not Western', thus lumping women in the third world as repressed individuals, which was identified much earlier than the issues mentioned above.

Relationship Between the Backlash and Criticisms to GAD in Japan

Criticisms to Gender Policies in Japan

Since the 1990s, criticisms by Japanese conservative mass media, conservative political parties and organizations, and some religious organizations to 'gender free' and 'explicit sex education', i.e. backlash,[3] have increased. The backlash in Japan began 10 years later than in the United States and targeted gender-equal 'regulations', 'gender free education' and 'sex education' (Kanai 2005).

To the best of the author's research, papers or essays critical of GAD did not exist in the 1990s. However, confrontation between gender advocates and conservative groups were common both in and outside of Japan. For example, it is well known that the *Love and Body Book for Adolescents* (Zaidan Houjin Boshi Eisei Kenkyukai 2002) targeting junior high and high school students and distributed since 2001, was criticized by the Education Committee of the House of Representatives in May 2002. Eriko Yamatani, a member of the House of Councilors from the Liberal Democratic Party, led the attack and as a result the book was withdrawn. In Paraguay, a research area of the author, an NGO received funding in 1998 from the United Nations Population Fund to promote Reproductive Health/Rights. A pamphlet was prepared on sex education using many illustrations so as to be easily understood by youth and rural people (Fujikake, 2003). The pamphlet included a simple illustration of a penis on the cover and targeted young people and their partners. However the pamphlets were withdrawn and burned by the then Minister of Public Health and Social Welfare, a devotee of *Opus Dei*[4] and Catholic power (ibid.). The conservative, or backlash movement, was very active in the United States, Japan and South America from the 1980 to 2000.

In Japan after 2000, a project team, 'Current State of Affairs Survey Project for Explicit Sex Education and Gender Free Education', was established (2005) with Shinzo Abe (present Prime Minister of Japan) from the Liberal Democratic Party as Chairman. The movement to exclude 'gender free' and 'gender' terminology from political and administrative sectors gained strength. At the same time, attacks against the anti-sexism movement, which this terminology fostered got combined with attacks to the constitution and the Fundamental Law of Education escalated (Japan Society for the Study of Materialism 2006). Conservative right wingers, such as from the 'Japan Conference' who had actively fostered the backlash, took the route to promote a neo-liberal 'gender equality' and used women's labour as a means to expand the market and win on the global economic front (ibid.). However, by using women's labour, their discussions have exerted unrelenting pressure on social welfare programmes which resulted in serious problems, such as the stratification of women, known as 'women-women disparity', and the ever spiraling decrease in the number of children. The backlash developed through the coexistence and mutually complementary relationship with the neo-liberal gender equality line (ibid.). The backlash foments attacks against an incompatible sex/gender dichotomy standard (e.g. gay, lesbian, bisexual, transgender, etc.).

Criticisms to Development Assistance Fields

Sato (2005) describes his views on GAD as follows:

> There are more than a few male staff, and even female staff, working for development assistance organizations who feel uncomfortable working with gender issues. It is not healthy for a man's mental health to be repeatedly reminded that 'I am taking

> advantage of gender inequality in Japanese society'; or a woman to think, 'Though I studied the social constructionism and gender in university, if I still want to buy a cute skirt and follow the gender norm, it is this because I lack gender awareness', which cuts the pleasure of shopping in half.

In addition, he states in his work, 'it is impossible to formally stand against the "troops" (public opinion of gender equality) parading a logic one dare not oppose' (ibid.).

Staff who prepare project planning in the field of practice are usually in charge of the overall project. Even though some may be competent in specific areas such as gender or environment, many must contract gender specialists or gender consultants to deal with gender issues. For example, JICA has two gender specialists as in-house consultants who deal with the various aspects of gender in a project. Each staff member has a different field of expertise therefore his/her specialty may not include gender. Then Sato's (ibid.) criticism is probably not appropriate in this situation.

In the book *Tekisutoshakaikaihatsu* (*Social Development Textbook: A New Course for Poverty Reduction*) by Sato (2007) there is no chapter dealing with gender. Sato (ibid.) comments on this in the 'Introduction':

> It was discussed during the editing stage of the book whether a textbook relating to social development without a chapter on gender was acceptable, or would raise doubts in some readers. It was decided among contributors not to include a specific chapter on gender reasoning that, 'gender considerations are indispensable in all sectors of social development therefore gender should be raised in each chapter, rather than in a specific chapter'. Actually every chapter of Part 1 and Part 2 in the book deals with considerations to socially disadvantaged people and a significant part is devoted to explain how women in socially disadvantaged situations can participate in the development process. Therefore, in this manner the book is regarded to adequately incorporate the gender perspective.
>
> There is an additional reason why a gender specific chapter was not intentionally created. Originally, the true nature of 'gender' was not to simply 'offer help to weak women', but to understand the social relationships between the two genders. However, the greater part of existing studies on social development are full of discussions in which gender issues are simply treated as women

issues. Many people express to some degree that this is wrong. In social development, 'gender', as well as 'social stratum', 'ethnicity' and 'regional disparity', must be understood from the point of view of 'disparity' and 'elimination', and if correct, it is not necessary to deal specifically with 'gender'. To include a chapter on gender in which gender is confused with women issues would not contribute to a balanced understanding of the general view of social development.

The explanation that the greater part of existing social development studies are filled with discussions in which gender issues are simply treated as women issues (Sato 2007), is considered an important viewpoint. There are numerous problems regarding gender issues which must be taken seriously from now on (e.g. issue specific themes, such as disasters and gender). Studies about vulnerability of women during disasters must be further developed and additional studies are needed on Men and Development (MAD). It must be taken into consideration that in many cases gender issues are targeted to women because they have many commonalities with women's issues due to gender disequilibrium, which imposes a heavy burden on women in developing, as well as in developed, countries (Figure 1).

Figure 1

Social Problems Related to Gender

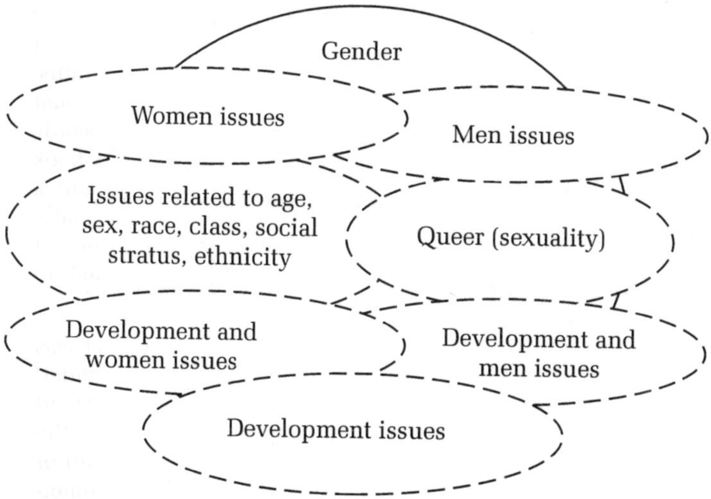

If Sato's (2007) comments are taken literally, it is understood that even though women issues have been discussed in existing social development studies, gender issues have not been. In other words, according to Sato's (ibid.) logic, women issues are discussed in books and papers on assistance but gender issues are not. If so, a textbook, which is a basic academic tool, must include a chapter on gender which discusses the original gender issues. Furthermore, the opinion, 'gender considerations are indispensable in all sectors of social development, therefore gender must be raised in each chapter, rather than in a specific chapter' (Sato 2007), may simplify multitiered problems in developing countries, which include complex cultural, religious, historical, class and social stratum aspects.

There were two sessions pertaining to gender in the National Conference (2010 Fall) of the Japan Society for International Development. One theme was 'Disability and Gender' and the other 'Development and Gender in Eastern Asia'. The following must be verified: whether only two of the total 35 sessions was an adequate representation, and whether any gender related analysis was done in the other social development sessions. As previously mentioned, one theme in the 2011 National Conference of the Japan Society for International Development was, 'Disaster Reconstruction and International Cooperation', however it made no mention of gender issues. Moreover, the 'Earthquake and Disaster Session' of the 2012 Spring Conference of the above society revealed that there had been no gender sensitive discussions. In other words, even though it is taken for granted that all social development sectors should as a matter of course have gender sensitive points of view (Sato 2007), the reality is different. Thus, although gender mainstreaming has been disseminated as a discourse, in fact there is no actual gender sensitive viewpoint or approach in Japanese society.

A Cue for Discussing the Re-examination of GAD Theory

Gender mainstreaming policy is thought to have had some positive outcomes. However, it is necessary to individually analyse the following: Sato's (2007) opinion that gender must be considered in social development projects as a matter of course; whether gender is, or is not, actually reflected in social development projects; whether gender issues are, or are not, resolved in the target society. It seems too drastic to conclude that, under gender mainstreaming if gender perspectives are incorporated in programmes but not in projects, this leads to including gender perspectives in all projects and programmes. It is necessary to examine the claim that no one is, or can, be responsible for gender because gender is obviously interdisciplinary and everybody's responsibility. This can be used as an excuse for the construction of the aforementioned discourse on 'gender has been mainstreamed'.

Below, an analytical framework will be offered as a tool to re-examine the discussion, after presenting the viewpoints of trainees from developing countries on whether or not gender mainstreaming has been accomplished.

Viewpoints of Trainees from Developing Countries: Has Gender Mainstreaming been Accomplished?

The author had the opportunity to be involved with the training course, 'Formation of Leaders Dedicated to Improving the Life and Status of Women', undertaken from 2007 to 2008, a collaboration between Kochi Women's University and JICA Shikoku.[5] Participants were individuals representing Afghanistan, Angola, Fiji, India, Mexico, Nepal, Nicaragua, Nigeria, Vietnam and Kenya for the 2007 fiscal year; and Afghanistan, Congo, Mexico, Nepal, Nicaragua, Sierra Leone and Vietnam for the 2008 fiscal year. The common language used was English.

During the workshop the question, 'Was gender mainstreaming accomplished?', was posed to the participants. Below are the participants' responses.

> Afghanistan (male): In Afghanistan women traditionally produce carpets and several NGOs have begun to offer assistance. However, in reality men take over the purchase and sale of carpets, leaving women without money. It is necessary to undertake a field survey on these gender problems.
>
> Fiji (female): Fiji is an island country and the trafficking of girls is increasing. However, trafficking has not become a topic of discussion. In addition, if a trafficking incident occurs, pursuit is hampered because the country is surrounded by sea, thus difficult to control. This problem is considered a new gender issue.

Mexico (female): Mexico has a machismo society (male superiority ideology) and women still face much violence. This is a problem we must keep working on. It cannot be said that gender mainstreaming has been accomplished in real society.

Nigeria (female): There is not enough financial assistance for women to start a business. It is necessary to establish a framework for women's independence.

Nicaragua (female): There is a clear gender division of labour, which means that women must dedicate themselves to domestic labour, while men work outside the household. Therefore, wish of women to participate in the public arena results in problems of violence from men towards women. Gender issues still firmly exist and countermeasures are necessary.

Vietnam (female): Cases of HIV/AIDS infection from husbands to wives are increasing. This is a new type of gender issue and the government and NGOs should intervene.

Kenya (female): In rural areas Female Genital Mutilation (FGM) still exists. I myself am promoting several initiatives through NGO activities to abolish FGM, however, it is not easy to change a cultural custom in a short term and women have limited access to education. The reality is that confronting the problem itself is difficult and external intervention, such as international cooperation, is necessary.

Nepal (female): Poverty in rural areas is very serious. Rural women rarely have access to education and there is no end to the cases of poor rural girls sold in India to work in brothels because their skin is lighter than Indians. Assistance from international society is necessary.

India (female): Dowry problems (Dowry death) can be seen every day in newspapers. It is a big gender problem in Indian society and it is necessary to debate on this from now on.

As seen above, participants from various countries pointed out that unsolved gender issues remain, new gender issues are arising, and projects related to gender are necessary. The participants are members of governmental organizations and NGOs, who analyse their society from their own perspective, so that their opinions may be different from the direct voice of the poor that are the target of assistance. Despite that, their opinions truthfully show the reality of each country. As seen in Figure 1, the issues discussed here can be considered women issues, however, when viewed that problems of discrimination and violence against women are the consequences of the relationship between a man and a woman, authority, social status and class discrimination, then it is more appropriate to consider them as gender issues.

As described earlier, gender mainstreaming has undoubtedly been generating positive outcomes. However, many interventions will be necessary in the future to correct disparities in the target society, or to correct disparities generated from structural problems. Due to this only the political term 'gender mainstreaming' has expanded to the development assistance programme or project level while existing real life problems are not receiving adequate attention, and new gender issues are arising. What is needed are analysis and assistance, with due consideration afforded to the views of women and children, who are usually at the bottom, and in a multifaceted way so that the people concerned do not become tragic heroines. It is necessary to repeatedly verify whether penetration of the political term without substance is presented as 'accomplished', when in fact it is the empty term 'gender mainstreaming has been accomplished' that has expanded alone.

Classifying GAD as a Tool for Re-examination of the Discussion

The author believes it necessary to reclassify GAD into the academic sphere and political and practical sphere, in order to resolve the above-mentioned discrepancies in the discussions. This is because GAD is lumped together as, 'GAD in research and practice sphere', and fallacies and/or problems arise. A large part of the criticisms observed in this paper are targeted to roles that are out of GAD's control. In other words, these criticisms are not valid. In order to resolve this issue, it is therefore proposed that GAD be classified in a narrow and a broad sense (Table 1). GAD in the narrow sense is institutionalized and (intentionally) 'depoliticized' during the creation of the strategic accord. GAD in the broad sense has developed in the deepened study of feminism and gender theory, and though very important, cannot be adopted in the fields of political and development practice.

As a result, Sato's (2005) criticism, 'social constructionism is understandable, however, it cannot be accepted emotionally', can be said to negatively view GAD in the broad sense. And this produces the observation that GAD in the broad sense isn't

Table 1

Criticisms to GAD Theory in Japan and a Tentative Study to Resolve Fallacies for the Reconstruction of GAD Theory

Classification	*Existing Problem*	*Criticism*	*Background*
GAD in the narrow sense, or institutionalized GAD	(1) People working in development assistance tend to internalize essentialism and the sex/gender dichotomy and become critical of GAD (Fujikake in this paper) (2) GAD, which was also institutionalized in Japan, is treated as an interdisciplinary subject while the term 'gender mainstreaming' has become widespread. As a result 'who' is responsible has become unclear (Chant 2007, Fujikake in this paper) (3) As a result of the institutionalization of GAD, the concept had become a mere shell and was depoliticized (Cornwall, Harrison & Wnitehead 2004: 2)	(1) Lack of consideration to historical facts, such as colonialism. Lack of consideration to the relationship between the neo-liberal economy, which is progressing on a global scale and exploitation (Fujikake 2005)	Assistance initiatives under UN or international society: questioning authority is problematic. Dominant development paradigm: premise that economic growth is absolute

Cont'd....

...Cont'd.

GAD in the broad sense	(1) There is a gap between the universal framework which GAD's analytical theory encompasses and the local context of the third world (Kumagai 2010)	(1) Social constructionism is understandable, however, cannot be accepted emotionally (Sato 2005). It is not healthy for a man's mental health to be repeatedly reminded that 'I am taking advantage of gender inequality in Japanese society' (ibid.)	Deepening of Agency Theory through feminism and post-colonial study is not adequately transmitted by studies. GAD is difficult to grasp. Uncomfortable
GAD theory reconstruction			Practice Theory is neither rationalized in GAD in the narrow sense nor in the broad sense

Source : Yoko Fujikake (revision of paper elaborated on October 10, 2008)
Quotations and references: Cornwall, Harrison & Wnitehead (2004), Chant (2007), Fujikake (2005), Kumagai (2010), Sato (2005, 2007)

cogently transmitting in the practice field the theory which was deepened by linking feminism and post-colonial studies. It is thought that people feel uncomfortable with GAD because it is difficult to understand.

As was already pointed out, the idea is that GAD has become an empty shell and depoliticized as a result of the institutionalization of GAD (Cornwall, Harrison and Whitehead 2004). However, depending on the interpretation of depoliticization this dictum could be very different. That is, whether depoliticization is interpreted as becoming an empty shell, or is the creation of a strategic accord or strategic compromise offering the first step towards discussion. The author would now like to take a stance to consider the creation of a strategic accord.

Though impossible to distinctly separate GAD in a narrow and a broad sense, it is necessary to classify it in this manner to avoid empty criticisms and discussions, so as to examine where the accumulated GAD theory studies can be used. In this way, Sato's (2005) criticism can be linked to a future task in GAD study, that is, for GAD researchers to competently transmit the deepening discussion by means of linking to feminism and post-colonial studies. The author proposes to reiterate that her intent is not to reproach GAD critics but to think constructively on how to deepen GAD research and studies without generating fallacies, in order to make GAD a study able to contribute to society. In the field of assistance (an area of GAD in the narrow sense), dissemination of a deepened gender concept by itself may not be enough, but at the same time, the dissemination of gender theory may be causing gender misunderstandings in assistance fields. Therefore, it is necessary to classify GAD theory in order to stimulate discussions. Though repetitious it bears stating that there is a blurred boundary between the narrow and the broad sense, but logically, a broad sense encompasses the narrow sense (Figure 1). This is a study and it is possible that this classification may be unnecessary when the fallacies are resolved.

As previously shown, a strategic accord or strategic compromise may be acceptable, but initially it is possible that the study approach (theory, technical terms, base values, and so on) is not acceptable in policy planning. Naturally, interpretation differs depending on one's values or historical viewpoint, and GAD advocates reliance on their own academic points of view. It is not constructive to indiscriminately criticize researchers and practitioners who support the GAD theory from different perspectives. The inarticulate expression of a GAD advocate's or practitioner's perspective, might be causing misunderstandings in readers or recipients, resulting in criticisms. However, these criticisms are connected, as on a Möbius strip (Fujikake 2011a), impeding the advancement of socially disadvantaged people (often women). In other words, criticizing GAD theory is tantamount to, whether one likes it or not, joining hands with the pro-backlash group.

Outcomes and Problems of GAD Theory

Not much time has passed since the study and practice arenas of WID, initiated in the 1970s, and GAD, which gained momentum in the 1980s, have been regarded and discussed as GAD theory. However, though the penetration of institutionalized GAD in developing countries, at least under 'United Nations' initiatives, has brought many positive outcomes, there are still problems to resolve. Ito (2003) states that transnational changes to prevent and abolish 'violence against women' were impossible without the rise of nationalism. In the same way, GAD theory would not have developed as it is today without the United Nations Decade for Women. Examined in this way, the United Nations and polities were necessary for the development of GAD theory.

Many researchers and practitioners have tried to respond to Mohanty's (1986) criticism, that GAD used the 'West' as the principal target of its theories and practice and designated others as 'not West', which lumps women in the third world as repressed individuals. The opinion that occidental feminism is ethnocentric and colonialistic has spawned a movement to study Asian feminism and/or Latin American feminism. There are studies which indicate that patriarchy and the gender division of labour must be understood in the individual local context. The author reiterates that GAD in the broad sense is a theory that encompasses GAD in the narrow sense (Figure 2), and problems in the field are reconstructing this theory.

Figure 2

Conceptual Diagram of the Relationship between GAD in the Narrow Sense and GAD in the Broad Sense

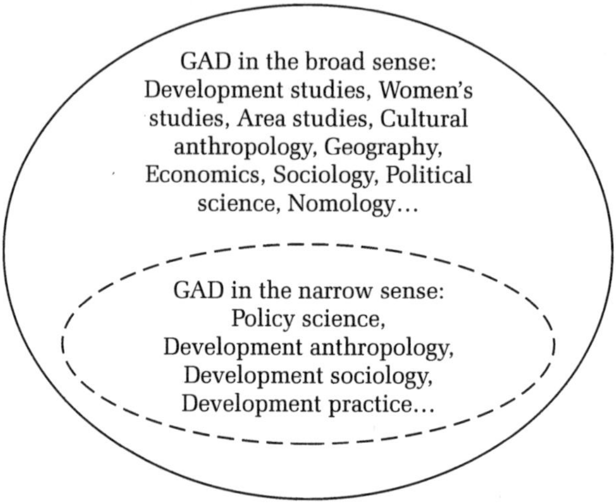

Outcomes of GAD in the Narrow Sense: Accomplishments of Gender Mainstreaming

A large number of gender sensitive development projects have been completed at present, and the importance of gender has been recognized to varying degrees, not only by the people in assistance organizations, but also by the very people in the target society.

The United Nations urges every country to establish, improve or reinforce its National Machinery to raise the social status of women, and details its own principle functions as follows: (1) help reflect women's needs and interests in government policies and plans, (2) seek grass-roots assistance, and (3) provide domestic and international information.[6] As institutional reform moves forward,[7] the linking of theory and practice is a major task that researchers and practitioners must work on together in the future.

In February 1991 in Japan, JICA presented suggestions on basic measures to incorporate WID viewpoints, and in 1997 Ochanomizi University (one of the two Women's National

University) established the 'Development and Gender Theory' graduate school masters course. In 1998, the number of female volunteers in the JOCV programme exceeded the number of male volunteers. Many people who studied in JICA or graduate schools in the past are still active in the GAD arena today. In June 1999, the Basic Act for Gender-Equal Society was approved and diverse actions have been completed to present. In 2013, Prime Minister Shinzo Abe proposed the 'Creation of a society where women can shine'.

Issues of GAD in a Broad Sense

With the deepening of feminism and gender studies, discussions have become more complicated and technical terms more difficult to understand. In addition, due to backlash, GAD has made people in the field of development practice feel uncomfortable. There have been the following criticisms to GAD – GAD means to question the relationship between men and women, the class or the social stratum, however, it is addressing only women issues; because GAD arose in developed countries, it is not possible to eliminate the tendencies of Orientalism in GAD.

In addition, it is necessary for GAD to continue confronting issues, such as, problems of other representation, questions of structural violence, limitations of the capitalist economy or neo-liberal values (Fujikake 2011b), that is, the problems of multinational enterprises, international labour, and environmental problems.

Braidotti et al. (1994) points out the need for GAD to find a way to resolve important issues such as how equal interrelationships can be constructed through the creation of an alliance transcending race, class, or the organization one is affiliated to and how excess consumption in the North can be transformed. In reality, the people who can create these alliances (e.g. those who participate in the United Nations or in international conferences and can construct networks), are those who are able to influence the policies of governments or international assistance organizations and who tend to be from a particular region or from a specific class. In many cases these people are women, and thus it is feared that this can lead to the re-creation of class or social stratum disparities in women (ibid.). At the same time, it is necessary to discuss actual problems and actions to prepare for future issues.

Trajectory of GAD Theory with Globalization

Base of the Pyramid (BOP) business and Corporate Social Responsibility (CSR) are buzzwords at the moment and Japanese companies have embarked in international cooperation ventures. Large companies quickly signed up and are now working on various projects, labeling them as 'contributions' to developing countries. Small and medium-sized companies are participating in BOP business centred training courses.[8] In step with this social trend, the Secretariat of Japan Overseas Cooperation Volunteers of JICA, created the Private Sector Partnership Volunteer Programme in July 2012, to 'support global human resource development and overseas venture development of private enterprise through the JOCV program'.[9] These initiatives must be sensitive to the cultural values and gender norms of the target country. On the other hand, contradictions are often found between neo-liberal values/norms and the purpose of grass-roots projects. Increasing tensions are foreseeable between the global business development of small, medium and large-sized companies in developing (emerging) countries and target regions. To avoid this conflict, it is necessary to classify and propose new values and norms in the narrow and in the broad sense using 'gender' and 'development' as keywords.

Tensions between development assistance and target sites as well as gender issues during the 1970s and 1980s, have been endlessly discussed. Boserup (1970) reported that development policies had generated unintended gender issues, and Elson (1995) documented women who were falling even deeper into poverty due to the development and structural adjustments implemented by the International Monetary Fund (IMF) and World Bank together with the government of a targeted developing country. Chant (2007) presents a case in Gambia where, though the women earned money through the progress made in gender mainstreaming in international society, men squandered the money, which resulted in yet another gender issue. Bain

(2010) points out, through research on workers in a fresh fruit-exporting sector in Chile (South America), that Global Partnership for Good Agricultural Practices (GAP), supposedly CSR, is creating a structural disparity for short-term female employees who don't receive adequate social security benefits. More field-based GAD research and studies with gender sensitive viewpoints, like the aforementioned examples, are required so as to present GAD issues in the narrow sense, as well as in the broad sense. GAD must be established as a study and practice sphere which connects theory with practice.

Conclusion: GAD as an Open Study

There is a wide gap between the dissemination of the political term, 'gender has been mainstreamed', and true equality achieved in the field. The Möbius strip connection between the discourse of 'accomplishment' and the arguments of pro-backlash groups must not impede the advancement of individuals who are structurally relegated to subordinate roles in societies with development assistance programmes. In order to rectify fallacies created by dissemination of the political term 'gender mainstreaming' and criticisms by backlash groups, it is first of all necessary to deepen the concepts of GAD in the narrow sense and GAD in the broad sense, as proposed in this paper, and work on new initiatives. Forty years of accumulated WID/GAD studies must not end here. More studies on GAD theory and practice are needed in Japan, and to achieve this, GAD must be examined more deeply through careful reflection of the various criticisms. At the same time, the labour force in Japan is shrinking and women are being roped into the labour market under the official slogan, 'Creation of a society where women can shine'. However, pay equity is not guaranteed and the household remains her responsibility. There are still very few women working for companies involved in decision-making, or those who are able to play a pivotal role in the development of the nation. There remain many problems to be resolved in order to attain a Japanese society where women can truly shine and we need the accumulated knowledge of WID/GAD.

NOTES

1. A Gender Equal Society is one in which people can be free from preconceptions or prejudices generated from expectations, such as 'a man should be...' or 'a woman should be...', and where people can participate regardless of gender but dependent upon one's personality.
2. In the early 1990s the term 'gender mainstreaming' had already been adopted in the 'decent work' of the International Labour Organization (ILO).
3. The term 'Backlash' was generalized after Susan Faludi (1992) used the term to refer to the reaction to feminism in her book *Backlash: The Undeclared War Against American Women*.
4. Abbreviation for Sociedad Sacerdotal de la Santa Cruz del Opus Dei, a worldwide Catholic organization founded by Spanish Priest José MaríaEscriva in 1928, and which means 'Work of God'. Its goals are to search for self-fulfillment and the sacred through one's professional life during their earthly existence. It received approval from the Pope in 1950 (Le Tourneau 1989).
5. Workshops were undertaken on 1 December 2007 and 3 December 2008.
6. In Japan, the Headquarters for the Planning and Promoting of Policies Relating to Women was established with the Prime Minister as its Administrative Chief in 1975, the International Women's Year. The Council for Gender Equality, in compliance with a government ordinance, was established in 1994, and the report on 'Vision of Gender Equality' was submitted in 1996. In the same year, the establishment of an advisory body based on this law, for the organizational and functional reinforcement of National Machinery, was clarified in the Plan for Gender Equality 2000. In 1997 the Council for Gender Equality, also based on this law, was established. The Basic Act for a Gender Equal Society was enacted in 1999 and the Commission for Gender Equality was established in 2001.
7. Initiatives for gender justice and equality have been undertaken in various countries beginning with the United Nations Decade for Women (1976–1985) and the Convention on the Elimination of All Forms of Discrimination against Women (CEDAW), which large numbers of countries have ratified

(186 countries as of 8 March 2011). The Japanese Government designates 'Assistance for Women/Gender' as an important task for the ODA and 'gender' viewpoints were reflected in the government plan presented at the World Summit on Sustainable Development held in Johannesburg, South Africa in August 2002. The United Nations Entity for Gender Equality and the Empowerment of Woman (UNWOMEN) was created on 1 January 2011, which is an integration of four previously existing bodies, the Division for the Advancement of Women (DAW), the International Research and Training Institute for the Advancement of Women (INSTRAW), the Office of the Special Adviser on Gender Issues and Advancement of Women (OSAGI) and the United Nations Development Fund for Women (UNIFEM).

8. The author was selected as jury member of the Sale Skills and Marketing Skills Training Crammer Final Presentation targeted to personnel of small and medium-sized companies, which Hachioji City consigned to the Metropolitan Industry Activation Association in fiscal year 2009. This included simulated training and a workshop on East Timor BOP business.
9. http://www.jica.go.jp/press/2012/20120710_01.html (Last accessed on 10 September 2012).

REFERENCES

Bain, Carmen (2010) 'Structuring the Flexible and Feminized Labor Market: Global GAP Standards for Agricultural Labor in Chile', *Signs: Journal of Women in Culture and Society* (Special Issue on Women and Agriculture), 35 (2).

Boserup, Ester (1970) *Women's Role in Economic Development*. New York: St. Martin's Press.

Braidotti, Rosi, Ewa Charkiewicz, Sabine Hausler and Saskia Wieringa (1994) *Women, the Environment and Sustainable Development: Towards a Theoretical Synthesis*. London: Zed Books.

Chant, Sylvia (2007) *Gender, Generation and Poverty: Exploring the 'Feminization of Poverty' in Africa, Asia and Latin America*. Cheltenham: Edward Elgar Publishing Limited.

Cornwall, A., E. Harrison and A. Whitehead (Eds) (2004) 'Repositioning Feminism in Gender and Development', *IDS Bulletin*, 35 (4).

Elson, Diane (1995) Male Bias in Macro-economics: The Case of Structural Adjustment. In Diane Elson (Ed.), *Male Bias in the Development Process*. Manchester: Manchester University Press.

Faludi, Susan (1992) *Backlash: The Undeclared War Against American Women*. New York: Three Rivers Press.

Fujikake, Yoko (2003) Paraguay nosonjosei no sei to seishokunikansuruishiki to sonohenka. In Naomi Nemura (Ed.), *Gender de yomukenko – Gender, sexuality*. Tokyo: Akashi Shoten. (In Japanese)

—— (2011a) Rokarunabunmyaku to gender no settenwomotomete. In Hiroshi Sato and Yoko Fujikake (Eds), *Kaihatsuenjo to jinruigaku*. Tokyo: Akashi Shoten. (In Japanese)

—— (2011b) Kikokugo no seinenkaigaikyoryokutaitachinoshakai-kokenkatsudonikansurukosatsu. In Seiji Utsumi (Ed.), *Kokusai Vorantiaron*. Kyoto: NakanishiyaShuppan. (In Japanese)

—— (2012) 'Kantogen', *International Society for Gender Studies* (Special Issue on Assistance and Gender), 10. (In Japanese)

Ito, Ruri (1995) Global feminism to tojokokujosei no undo. In Yoshikazu Sakamoto (Ed.), *Sekaiseiji no kozohendo*. Tokyo: Iwatani Shoten. (In Japanese)

—— (2003) Komneto. In Mackie Vera (Ed.), *Globaruka to Gender Hyousyo*. Tokyo: OchanomizuShobou. (In Japanese)

Japan Society for the Study of Materialism (Ed.) (2006) *Gender gainengahirakushikai*. Tokyo: Aoki Shoten. (In Japanese)

Kanai, Yoshiko (2005) Gender Backlash no Kozu to Naimen. Asia Taiheiyo niokeru gender to heiwagaku. Yokohama: Ferris University. Retrieved on 1 December 2008 from http://home.att.ne.jp/wood/akira/ferris/kyodoken/index_kenkyukai.htm. (In Japanese)

Le Tourneau, Dominique (1989) *L'OpusDei*. France: CollectionQue sais-je. (In French)

Mohanty, Chandra Talpade (1986) Under Western Eyes: Feminist Scholarship and Colonial Discourses. In Anne McClintock (Ed.), *Dangerous Liaisons: Gender, Nation, and Postcolonial Perspectives*. Minneapolis: University of Minnesota Press.

Muramatsu, Yasuko (1997) Josei to kaihatsu. In Jun Nishikawa (Ed.), *Shakaikaihatsu*. Tokyo: Yuhinkaku. (In Japanese)

Sato, Hiroshi (2005) *Kaihatsuenjo no shakaigaku*. Kyoto: Sekai Shisosha. (In Japanese)

—— (2007) *Tekisutoshakaikaihatsu*. Tokyo: Nihon Hyoronsha. (In Japanese)

Tanaka, Yumiko (1995) Kaihatsu to josei. In Japan International Cooperation Agency (Ed.), *Kokusai kyoryokugairon*. Tokyo: JICA. (In Japanese)

Tinker, Irene (1990) *Persistent Inequality*. Oxford: Oxford University Press.

ZaidanHoujinBoshiEiseiKenkyukai (2002) *Love and Body Book for Adolescents*. Tokyo: ZaidanHoujinBoshiEiseiKenkyukai. (In Japanese)

3

Study on 'Gendered Membership' in China's New Urbanization Reform

An Interpretative Framework with Feminist Perspective

WANG XIAOLI AND ZHANG CHAO

After the 1995 Fourth World Conference on Women (FWCW) held in Beijing, when the Chinese government signed two documents of the United Nations, 'Programme of Action' and the 'Beijing Declaration', Chinese women's organizations started to promote gender equality in all levels of government. Terms of gender equality have been written into China's relevant laws, including the 'Marriage Law', 'Land Management Law', 'Rural Land Contract Law', and 'Women's Rights and Interests Protection Law'. Since the implementation of the Household Contract Responsibility System (hereinafter HCRS or land contracting), the patrilineal family as a unit of land management recovered and women's participation in productive labour again returned to the private sphere of the family. In national discourse, equality and rights were introduced into laws and policies, which was considered as a big step forward, while in the private sector, it got very limited recognition that oppression against women also exacerbated women's inequality. In reality, due to changes in patrilineal marital relationship (married, divorced, widowed, etc.), women encounter the situation of landlessness repeatedly. Since the first round of land contracting (15 years of fixed tenure) in early 1980s, married women need to wait a few years or even never get re-distribution of land in husband's village (Li and Xi 2006); after the second round of land contracting (30 years of fixed tenure) in mid 1990s, this phenomenon has become very common (for those who got married after the second round of contracting) (Zhang and Liu 2005).

Since the 1990s, along with the advance of China's urbanization, the trend of rural land expropriation and land stock cooperation has been increasing and women's legal land rights re-gained concerns. In land contracting and land transfer, women's impaired rights in decision-making were often overshadowed under their patriarchal family and failed to arouse enough attention even among women themselves. But in land expropriation and stock cooperation, landed property became capital compensation or stock rights, to be redistributed in the community. The legal land rights of *Nong Jia Nv* (hereinafter the 'left-over women'), which includes uxorilocally-married women (women who remain living in their birth village even after marriage), divorced, widowed and even single women of marriageable age, all being statuses outside of a virilocal marital relationship, have often been expropriated at community level. In practice, it is a titled 'membership' issue. Women's membership is often based on their patrilineal birth right. After getting married, their membership turns to be linked with their virilocal marriage. Uxorilocally-married women who remain living in their birth village even after marriage, due to the residency policy or personal reasons, often get excluded from the redistribution of land compensation and from the land stock reform. The circumstances of divorced and widowed women after moving back to live in their patrilineal village is the same. In some villages, single women in their, early thirties, also encounter similar expropriations. Hence the term of 'left-over women' reveals that in practice 'membership' is an androcentri configuration, a 'gendered membership'. In the past decade, along with an increase of 13 per cent in China's urbanization ratio, increase in women's land rights expropriation per cent also reached 13 per cent (ACWF 2011). Thus the question arises as to how is women's marital status translated into a village citizenship criterion? This paper aims at providing an interpretative framework of the 'gendered membership', in feminist, historical and institutional narratives.

Literature Review

In current studies, the above phenomena is commonly regarded as a women's land issue. Researchers are committed to figure out different forms of gender inequality in China's land policy implementation and its consequences. The basic premise of these studies is that women play a more and more significant role in the country's economic development. One type of research is theoretically based on the position of women, from the perspective of welfare and justice, and concerns the phenomena of 'feminization of poverty' (Hu, Guo and Dong 2008), emphasizing the protection of women's legal land rights contributing to the achievement of the state's goal in poverty reduction (Zhu 2000). Another study is based on theories of 'women's experiences' and concerns women's land access and its relevance to agricultural production and food security. This 'efficiency' perspective gained more attention after China's joining the WTO (Lin and Qiu 2001). Whether it is based on the position of women or on women's experiences, in those studies, women are a research object often seen as homogenous group. The core is to explore how the public administration goals, such as efficiency and fairness, are affected by variables of gender inequality in property relationship. Analysis focuses on the interface of gender relations at the household level and strengthens the role of women as passive victims, but does not go into the explanation of why one must distinguish between family's common property and individual rights (Sargeson 2008). And we rarely hear women express themselves in any of these studies.

Stivers first proposed a feminist perspective in public administration research to review the patriarchal social structure (Stivers 1991) beyond the theoretical basis of women's experience and position. What China's rural women encountered in land expropriation and land stock reform, is neither merely a women issue nor a land issue, rather it reflects a set of andocentric configuration based on gender inequality and power relations in private and public spheres. These result in structural constraints for women's individual access to their land, limiting opportunities for women to participate in political and public affairs. Along with land expropriation and land stock reform, land and other village assets increase in value because of which villagers attempt to limit wealth distribution by voting to expunge the rights of 'left-over' women. Though legally women have equal land rights in law, when it comes to the new term 'membership', there is no legal definition yet to qualify.

Liberal scholars who follow Thomas Marshall's definition of citizenship emphasize that those with the status of citizen enjoy rights, including civil rights to justice and property, political rights to join in public deliberation and governance, and the social rights to public goods that ensue from citizens' exercise of civil and political rights (Sargeson and Yu 2010). Republican theorists have interpreted citizenship as active participation in the political life of the community. More recent scholarship synthesizes these theoretical approaches by examining the co-constitution of rights and political engagement (Gaige 2008). As Ruth Lister (2003) puts it, 'citizenship as rights enables people to act as political agents, but it is through political engagement that people achieve citizenship entitlements'.

In China's practice, village autonomy adopted citizenship rules that make women's membership conditional on their marriage to local men, thereby perpetuating men's control of collective and household wealth. Membership rights claimed by villagers are looked into on behalf of village committee by village representatives of which men constitute most of the decision-makers and voters. They make the rules, control most property and earn most supporters and this risks overlooking 'gendered membership' as a means. Women were divided, rather than united, however, by their status of different marital relationship. Under such circumstances, in communities and within a patrilineal family, it often incurs conflicts over compensation and stockholder entitlement between the 'left-over' women and the 'married-in' women. In general, women are becoming more economically and virilocal marital dependent, which display greater gender inequality at family and community levels.

An Interpretative Framework of 'Gendered Membership'

In rights perspective, 'membership' has different political and economic meanings in the domain of villagers' autonomy, rural land requisition and collective property or land stock cooperative restructuring. The state's land extraction and rural land stock reform are often challenged by the clarification of 'membership'. After China's reform and opening up, *hu ko* (residence), birth village, land rights and permanent residence are often inconsistent. Under the impact of urbanization and industrialization, village committee and rural economic organizations increasingly get separated; land property gets linked with members' contract land rights while *hu kou* or residency contains access to village collective benefits and rights to participate in public affairs, such as social welfare and maternity services (earlier known as obligation to obey the family planning policy). In terms of villagers' autonomy, it also means the voting rights (Bo 2013). Under the village autonomy, in practice, membership criteria differs from place to place: as law-based criteria linking individual's membership to one's residence and land rights; while in some village autonomy-made criteria, linking it to one's patrilineal birth right and virilocal marital right. The latter brings about the issue of the so-called 'left-over women'.

By policy analysis and multi-case study this article provides an interpretative framework of the 'gendered membership', in dimensions of gendered difference sequence, gendered village governance and patriarchy traditional rules in an urbanizing rural economy and society. Two cases selected, Bai village of Hubei province, located in a new urban zone, represents the land expropriation case; and Na village of Guangxi province, in the newly established development zone, represents the land stock reform case. In both cases, women whose *hu kou* is retained in their birth villages, mostly the uxorilocally married, divorced or widowed, encountered the same empty 'membership', with completely no contract land-based rights, such as contract land compensation, contract land stock share, rehousing land distribution and with no social welfare and other citizenship rights or services. In both cases, the 'left-over women' not only expressed their rights appeal, but also caused attention and got response from the high-level government departments, including the All China Women's Federation (ACWF).

The Gendered Difference Sequence in an Urbanizing Rural Economy and Society

From the perspective of 'driven mechanism' and 'spatial mode' to understand China's urbanization, its prominent features include government led large-scale planning that is overall-driven. Sine rural land is collectively owned, it must be turned to national ownership for construction and industrialization purposes. Expropriation becomes inevitable despite rural and civil societies not yet being in a condition for spontaneously becoming urbanized. As Li, Chen and Liu (2012) summarized, there are seven types of driven mechanisms: the establishment of Development Zones, the New City or District Construction, Urban Expansion, Urban Renewal, Construction of the Central Business District, Township and Village Industrialization. The first five types are accompanied by the state's land extraction. The last two modes, Township and Village Industrialization, involve the land use change from agrarian to industry purpose. This typical Chinese urbanization brought a series of changes in rural economy and society, in which the gendered difference sequence remains controversial.

According to the Sixth National Census and Statistical Yearbook data, China's urbanization rate has reached 47.63 per cent and the proportion of non-agricultural employment reached 62.8 per cent. Compared with 1985, the number of the country's administrative villages decreased by 3,42,000 in 2009. By the end of 2012, the national rural land transfer area was about 270 million mu (18 million ha), accounting for 21.5 per cent of household contract land. Along with non-agricultural employment of rural population, challenges for 'membership' identification were emerging, such as the 'separation of population and residency' or 'rural empty residency' (namely, migrant rural population living in the urban areas but with rural residency), and 'dual residency' (someone who owns both urban and rural residencies illegally). This has resulted because of the *hu kou* system which was launched by the Chinese government in 1958. As a household registration system, it was introduced to facilitate the centrally-planned industrialization during the reform period (1978 to the present). By 1983 as a result of separation of township administration from the rural economy, as a general trend, rural population started to migrate to non-agricultural industries in urban areas. The decline of rural population was accompanied by the increase of urban population (by populations' living places, not by *hu kou*). In 2010, percentage of urban population reached 49.68 per cent. In contrast with the population migration, urban residency has been under strict control due to the Urban-Rural *hu kou* system, which incurred the increasing separation of population and residency (see Chart No. 1, 2 and 3 for a clearer understanding). Women, who married urban residents, were not allowed to move their *hu kou* to cities, due to the strict Urban-Rural *hu kou* system. In such marital relations, women have no other choice but to remain at their birth place residence. Categorizing a woman as 'married out' resulted in her expatriation and what Augustine-Adams (2002), in a comparative study of marital expatriation laws, dub as 'civil annihilation'.

Chart 1

China's Population Trend

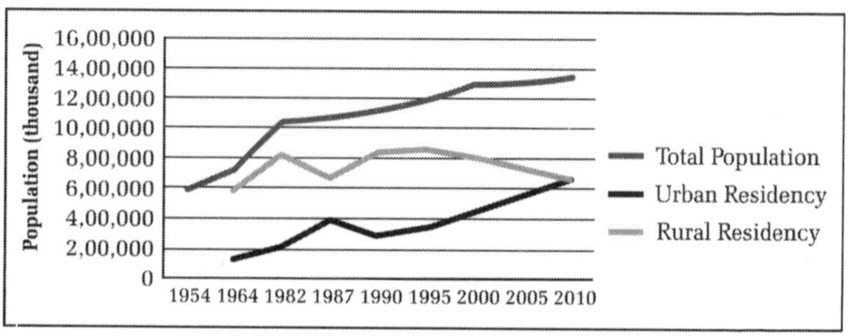

Chart 2
Urban Population Percentage

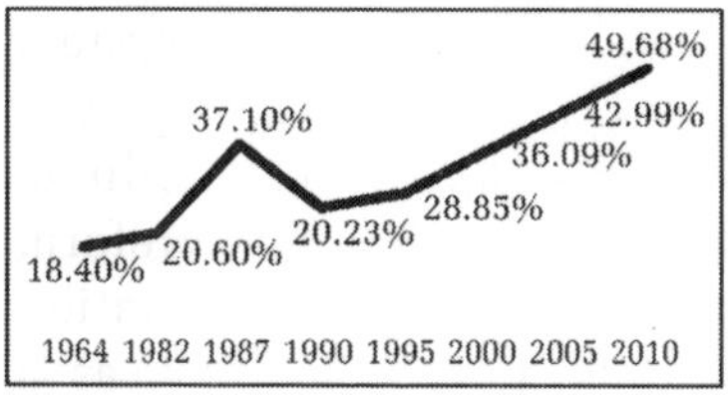

Chart 3
Separation of Population and Residency (SPR) Percentage

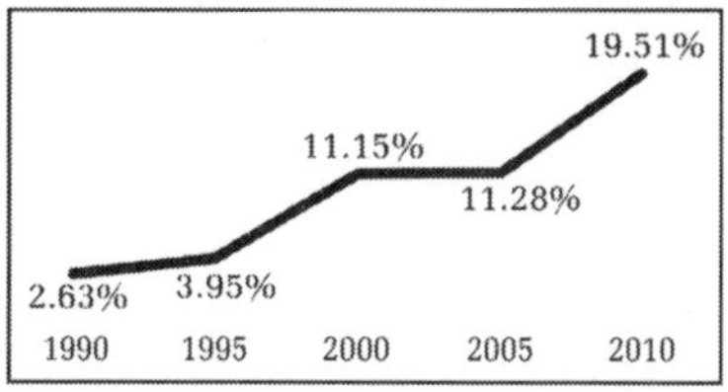

Source: National Census and Statistical Yearbook Data in year 1954, 1964, 1982, 1990, 2000, 2010

Note: 1 per cent of the national population sample survey data in year 1987, 1995, 2005

In China's context, at the macro-level, urbanization is seriously lagging behind in industrialization and economic growth (Gu and Liu 1996) while the quality of urbanization and the leading role of development of the countryside is not strong (Zhou 2001). Furthermore the Urban-Rural *hu kou* system has been criticized as an obstacle to the New Urbanization or the Urban-Rural Integration.

In 1985 the Communist Party of China (CPC), Central Committee and State Council issued a document that allowed farmers to migrate into the city for doing small business or providing a variety of services. During this period, the township and village industrialization got supported by the state. In the village, small and labour-intensive enterprises flourished. Village enterprises' community or geopolitical preferences tend to offset their gender preferences (Jin 1998). Therefore it absorbed a number of rural women as cheap labour force. Jin (1998) pointed out, that women are mainly concentrated in low-income rural enterprises, and distributed in the pipeline. Female labour from three survey villages working in the township enterprises, account for 77.56 per cent, 79.15 per cent and 69.87 per cent of the labour force, higher than men by 19.81 per cent, 13.15 per cent and 9.53 per cent respectively. In such industrialized villages, when a woman marries, unlike the virilocal marriage, she would choose to remain in her birth *hu ko* for a wage job and better living. The terms *Shang Jia* (upward-marriage) and *Xia Jia* (downward-marriage), represent the above phenomena. If a woman gets married with a man in a less-industrialized or less-urbanized village, it is seen as a 'downward' marriage and vice versa. In a downward marital relation, at her patrilineal village, normally only a woman's *hu kou* is retained, but it is devoid of any collective benefits attached with her 'membership' in the village. If her contract land rights remain, it is usually under the entitlement of her father's family while in a number of villages, it is quite common that her contract land is reallocated to another newly married-in woman at community or family level. Researchers blame the flaw in the current Land Management Law (Wang and Li 2013), as it is a male-headed household registration system, because of which the 'left-over womens' legal contract land rights are affected by abuse of power in patrilineal family and gender inequality at private and public sphere.

In the late 1990s, rural industries began to go bankrupt or were privatized, often in a manner that allowed village cadres to dismiss those 'left-over women' as their prime targeted group. Unemployed women often have no choice but to migrate for waged work opportunities in urban areas. In both 'feminization of agriculture' and in 'rural industrialization', rural women played an important role as 'labour force reservoir' for both development of urban and rural industries. It is a restructuring process of rural economy and society, as well as a reallocation process of collective resources. 'Non-agricultural labour migration produced gendered sequence, in forms of lower female occupations and reshaping new gender inequality interests structure' (Jin 1998). Jin (ibid.) analysed how rural industrialization reproduced the gender hierarchy and how it got institutionalized through industry organizations. However in Jin's study, women were surveyed as homogenous group. Our study points that it is necessary to distinguish the 'left-over women' from the 'left-behind women', because ever since China's opening up and reform started along with the flourishing, declining, and reviving of village entrepreneurs, the gender hierarchy also became segregated. As rural women's legal membership rights as individuals are unguaranteed, their access to community resources is based on their virilocal marital relationship, in particular the access to contractible land, housing land and other collective services such as opportunities for rural industrial employment. The housing land, in many rural communities, is called 'ancestral land' or 'ancestor's house'. It is an institutionalized patrilineal family-centred inheritance system. In 1981's first round of land contracting, rural China's housing land was not involved from the beginning. In many villages, daughters can never get the inheritance of housing land. Only in households without sons could one daughter, conceptualized and institutionally treated as a proxy son, marry uxorilocally and retain a village membership. According to the villagers whom we surveyed, even if an ancestor's house collapsed, there is definitely no one who will dare to occupy it. In contrast, for some families with more sons, men can explore new housing land as much as needed. In early 1990s, the village committee started to apply for permit of housing land use, entitled as 'rural collective ownership land'. The legislation of housing land, paradoxically, expropriated the left-over women's legal individual rights.

The Gendered Village Governance and Traditional Rules in Patriarchal Rural Society

Na Village

Economic Development Zone (EDZ) of Nanning City, established in 1992, got approved as a state-level economic and technological development zone in 2001. In 2012, it covered an area of 504 square kilometres consisting of 3 townships, 22 villages and 5 urbanized communities, with a population of 2,50,000. Of this, agricultural population accounted for 26 per cent. In 2005, the EDZ got 3,000 mu (200 ha) of construction land quota, including the total area of 2,600 mu of Na village. Before the land expropriation, villagers relied on agricultural income and there were no village entrepreneurs. As land compensation, an average family of five persons receives compensation of 12 million yuan (1,97,880 USD, at present exchange rate); in addition, there is rental income of about 17,500 yuan per year based on the local 'one residency, one rehousing villa' compensation rule, with community collective stock revenue. As the village cadre claimed proudly, '*other villages are jealous, expecting the government to extract their land*'.

In 2005, there were 20 'left-over women' in Na village. In 1981's first land contracting, as unmarried woman (or daughter), they all gained contracted land. In the following years, only Group 2 took back their land to do reallocation, but with no written record (See Table 1). In Na village, villagers are strongly against the married woman living with her father's family, which is deemed to bringing 'bad luck', or 'no son in the family'. According to villagers' survey, in 1980s, there were two married daughters living in the village who were expelled from the village and forced to build their houses in controversial forestland. In Na village, even for those with only daughters, uxorilocal marriage is not permitted. Based on their traditional rules, their nephews should take responsibilities of looking after the elderly. If there is no nephew, then it is a custom to adopt a cousin's son. After 2000, 7 of 20 left-over women built houses in controversial forestland or in their father's self-exploited barren land. None of 20 'left-over women' got rehousing settlement. Urbanization put them in homeless status since then.

Table 1

Rehousing Land Area in Na Village

Village groups	*Approved area of land for rehousing(m^2)*	*Area of land in use for rehousing construction(m^2)*	*Population resettled*
Group 1	14,421	5,776	308
Group 2	11,172	4,488	204
Group 3	13,940	5,038	229
Group 4	5,557	1,892	86

Bai Village

In Bai village, located at the urban centre, land rights have been transferred in below three stages: farmer wasteland shares and collective rights of use from 1950s to 1970s; 1983–1985 with only two years of land contracting (Household Contract Responsibility System HCRS); and 1985 to present when contracted lands are being reclaimed and reallocated by village committee in form of land-use right rent. In a compulsory approach, villagers' land-use rights (contracted land and housing land) got into trading market. In 2011, the village leader issued a land stock cooperative reform plan, which divided all villagers into 21 categories, including 11 categories of villagers as the stockholder, the other 10 categories excluded from the stock share. The total population of who were entitled to 'membership' rights, dropped from 6,000 (originally by residency) to 2,368. 'Membership' share was further divided into two categories: the basic stock (10 shares), and the specific stock (shares ranging from 2 to 9), while villagers with specific membership got subdivided into 10 groups. See Table 2 for a clearer picture.

Table 2

The Membership Criterion of Bai Village in Land Stock Reform

	Membership Criterion	*Y=1 : -/N=0*				*Score*
		R	*B*	*L*	*C*	
	Villagers with Membership					
1.	Bai villagers, with full access to collective welfare, and their children	Y	Y	Y	Y	4
2.	Former village members who were turned to own urban residency (as compensation for their contracted land expropriation), with no urban social welfare, unemployed and remain living in Bai Village	N	N	N	Y	1
3.	The uxorilocal husband in family with son, with permission from previous village cadres, removed residency to Bai Village, participated in farming activities, with full rights of Bai's welfare, fulfilled village duties (such as agricultural tax)	Y	Y	N	Y	3
4.	The uxorilocal husband and children in family without sons, signed a maintenance agreement (civil servant expected)	Y	Y	N	Y	3
5.	Female villagers with disabilities	Y	Y	Y	Y	4
6.	The widowed villager who marries in for the purpose of children care, the married-in husband is allowed to bring one child to Bai Village	Y	Y	Y	Y	3
7.	Male villager who has only one child after widowed or divorced, the married-in woman is allowed to bring one child	Y	Y	N	Y	3
8.	Villagers who are in professional schools, universities or acting compulsory military service	N	N	–	N	0

Cont'd...

...Cont'd

9. Former male villagers, removed residencies, with official employment. While their left behind spouses and children, live in Bai village, fulfilled village duties, with uninterrupted access to village welfare	N	Y	N	Y	2
10. Male villager marries urban woman who is unemployed, and their policy allowed children	N	Y	N	Y	2
11. Former villagers, employees returned with permission from previous village cadres, and their children	Y	N	N	Y	2
Villagers without membership					
12. Children of the former villagers who were recruited as non-agricultural employees	N	N	N	N	0
13. Illegal adoptions of children, and children born in violation of family planning policy (second child after 1st Jan, 2009, third child after 1st Jan, 1984)	Y	Y	N	N	2
14. Villagers determined the death before the issue of this policy	–	–	–	–	–
15. All population with empty membership	Y	–	N	N	1
16. Formal villagers with social welfare after recruitment	N	N	N	N	0

Note: 1. R=Residency B=Birth-right L=Land-right C=Residence Contribution
2. Law-based Scoring ('Y'=law-based; 'N'=against law; '–'=irrelevant)

From feminist perspective, the above 'membership' criteria are gender-based. The first category of female villagers and their children, as defined in term 2, 9 and 10 (see Table 2), are entitled to 'membership' unconditionally, based on their virilocal marital relationship. Their law-based scoring is merely 1–2. The second category of female villagers, as being out of their virilocal marriage dependence, are fully excluded from membership entitlement, such as the uxorilocal married, divorced, widowed women, as in term 19 and 20. The precondition for their membership retainment is linked with their physical and marriage status, as listed in term 3, 4, 5 and 6. The 'membership criterion' based on Bai village's self-governance is androcentrically configured. Bai's membership criteria manifested gender inequality by converting virilocal marriage custom into village governance rules, limiting distribution of collective stock and mandating women's marital expatriation. Function of laws issued to enhance gender equity was limited by village autonomy policies that continued to presume patrilineal predominance in public decision-making and production.

It is found that understandings of the 'membership' differs from one to other among village cadres and villagers. There is no uniform criterion, not to mention the rule of law. Their key arguments are divided into three categories: one is residency-based – membership should be based on one's *hu kou*; second view relies on village's self-governance – with permission from the village representatives and village party members, one can gain 'membership'; and third is defined by the 'villagers' welfare', namely, linking one's rights with other collective rights. However, other collective rights were determined by the village committee. The 'married-out' women who remained living in Bai village, in its residency reform in 2003, were excluded unconditionally. As their marriage and family can no longer provide important support, the 'left-over women', deploy their rightful social movement using discourses of law and policies.

Conclusion

In the process of China's top-down driven urbanization, rural society transformation is seriously lagging behind in industrialization and economic growth. A large proportion of rural population is absorbed by non-agricultural employment. Numerous amount of rural land has been expropriated for non-agricultural use or undergoing stock cooperative reform. The above changes are followed by the increasing value of village 'membership'. In this context, it brought about increasing cases of 'separation of population and residency', which in turn, makes the 'membership' clarification more challenging. In the meantime, rural society is still under patriarchal structure, the virilocal marriage pattern and the patrilineal system of contracted land distribution and inheritance, are still playing an important role. It formed an institutionalized barrier for rural women's marriage or employment-oriented migration and opened the space for villages' self-governance. Gender inequalities in civil, political, economic and social entitlements widened after the land expropriation and stock cooperative reform since 1990s. Scholars started to talk about the crisis and class stratification of rural society, while the gender stratification is rarely addressed.

Women's 'membership' in a village collective often is debated (Sargeson and Yu 2010). The village's self-governance, acts as an institutionalizing and rationalizing means, from virilocal custom to marital expatriation, which reproduced the gendered membership. Patriarchal ideology and discourse are taken as a new weapon to rationalize its illegal self-governance. The local township as the accountable government institute, according to the village self-governance law, should take responsibility for correcting village governance. While in reality, the gendered difference sequence in urbanizing rural society, together with the gender inequality, village governance, play a greater role as the value of rural land has been increasing. Local governments' failure to enforce legislation, facilitated the 'majority voting' taking on a new significance, in which the village committee and patriarchy have the decision-making power. Some scholars even argued that the township government and village self-governance system created at the time, in other words, was no longer suitable for the development of rural society and the market economy (Kuhn 2002). Thus arise the questions of should village committee focus on democratization and the representation of interests in the political sphere or collective organization in the economic sphere as well and how to make the local government a real accountable agency in village self-governance?

Women's residency became virilocal marriage-based. Women's rights of contracted land and housing land became patrilineal household-based, non-independent land rights. And women's 'membership' rights turn to be based on virilocal marriage and patrilineal household. In practice, many village committees have adopted a criterion that make women's 'membership' conditional to their marriage to local men, thereby perpetuating men's control of collective and household wealth. The gendered stratification, does not just mean male and female hierarchy, but emphasizes on male-centred marriage and inheritance system as the foundation of women's division. At community level, women's individual 'membership' has been thoroughly invaded, and only married women get rights under the guise of their virilocal marital relationship. With the policy of constructing a 'New Socialist Countryside' and the end of agricultural tax, not only are women deprived of their legal land rights, along with denial of women's legal membership, but also causes the illegal deprivation of women's social welfare in medical service, the aged care, and family planning services, their access to improved infrastructure, education facilities, and the resettlement into better housing, as well as women's participation in public and political affairs. Without urgent and proper intervention, advocates of new urbanization reproduce injustice and gendered class rather than providing the theoretical tools and language with which to address equality. There is an urgent need for county-level and above governments to monitor villages' land compensation distribution and land stock cooperation reform, to ensure that women equally participate in, and benefit from new urbanization.

Further, along with China's new urbanization, we see an emerging trend of the 'left-over womens' rightful resistance against the illegal village autonomy and the patriarchal system, to defend their individual legal rights and civil entitlements. It is belief in collective socio-economic justice, rather than a desire for individual civil and political rights, that distinguishes political thought and action in China (Perry 2008).

REFERENCES

All China Women's Federation (ACWF) (2011) 'Di san ci zhon guo fu nv she hui di wei diao cha (Executive Report of the 3rd Survey on the Status of Chinese Women)', *Fu nv yan jiu lun cong (Collection of Women's Studies)*, 6.

Augustine-Adams, K. (2002) 'With Notice of the Consequences: Liberal Political Theory, Marriage, and Women's Citizenship in the United States', *Citizenship Studies*, 6 (1).

Bo, L.Z. (2013) 'Ji ti de chong gou: Zhu jiang san jiao zhou di qu nong cun chan quan zhi du de yan bian – yi 'wai jia nv' wei li

(Collective Reconstruction: The Evolution of the Pearl River Delta Region in Rural Areas – Case on 'Married-Out-Women' Controversy)', *Open Times*, 3.

Gaige, M.P. (2008) *The Future of Citizenship*. Cambridge, MA: MIT Press.

Gu, S.Z. and C.J. Liu (1996) 'Cheng zhen hua xiao ying yu sheng yu xing bie pian hao (Theoretical Thinking and Policy Options on Chinese Migration and Urbanization)', *Zhong guo ren kou (Population Research)*, 20 (3).

Hu, Y.K., W. Guo and D. Dong (2008) 'Zhi shi pu xi, hua yu quan li yu fu nv fa zhan – guo ji fa zhan zhong de she hui xing bie li lun yu shi jian (Knowledge Genealogy, Discourse Power and Women's Development – Gender Theories and Practices in International Development)', *Nan jing da xue xue bao (zhe xue. Ren wen ke xue. She hui ke xue ban) Journal of Nanjing University (Philosophy, Humanities and Social Sciences)*, 45 (4).

Jin, Y.H. (1998), 'Fei nong hua guo cheng de nong cun fu nv (The Process of Non-agricultural Rural Women)', *She hui xue yan jiu (Sociological Studies)*, 5.

Kuhn, P.A. (2002) *Origins of the Modern Chinese State*. Stanford: Stanford University Press.

Li, Q., Y.L. Chen and J.M. Liu (2012) 'Zhong guo cheng zhen hua 'tui jin mo shi' yan jiu (On the 'Development Mode' of Chinese Urbanization)', *Zhong guo she hui ke xue (Social Sciences in China)*, 7.

Li, Y. and Y.S. Xi (2006) 'Married Women's Rights to Land in China's Traditional Farming Areas', *Journal of Contemporary China*, 15 (49).

Lin, Z.B. and G.J. Qiu (2001) 'Quan qiu hua zai nong ye ling yu dui zhong guo fun v de qian zai ying xiang (The Latent Influence of Globalization on Chinese Women in the Agricultural Sector)', *Fu nv yan jiu lun cong (Collection of Women's Studies)*, 1.

Lister, R. (2003) *Citizenship: Feminist Perspectives*. New York: NYU Press.

Perry, E.J. (2008) 'Chinese Conceptions of 'Rights': From Mencius to Mao and Now', *Perspectives on Politics*, 6 (1).

Qian, W.R. and Y.C. Mao (2005) 'Zhong guo nong cun fu nv tu di quan li wen ti de shi zheng yan jiu (An Empirical Study of Land

Rights of Rural Women in China)', *Zhe jiang da xue xue bao (ren wen she hui ke xue ban) Journal of Zhejiang University (Humanities and Social Sciences)*, 35 (5).

Sargeson, S. (2008) 'Women's Property, Women's Agency in China's New Enclosure Movement: Evidence from Zhejiang', *Development and Change*, 39 (4).

Sargeson, S. and S. Yu (2010) 'Land Expropriation and the Gender Politics of Citizenship in the Urban Frontier', *The China Journal*, 64.

Stivers, C. (1991) 'Toward a Feminist Perspective in Public Administration Theory', *Women and Politics*, 10 (4).

Wang, X.L. and H.Y. Li (2013) 'Cheng zhen hua jin cheng zhong fu nv tu di quan li de shi jian luo ji (Women's Land Rights in Practice in the Process of Urbanization: A Case Study of 'Uxorilocally Married Women' in Nanning)', *Fu nv yan jiu lun cong (Collection of Women's Studies)*, 6.

Zhang, L.X. and C.F. Liu (2005) 'Cong xing bie shi jiao kan zhong guo nong cunt u di tiao zheng zhong de gong ping wen ti – dui quan guo 1199 ge nong hu he 2450ge cun de shi zheng diao cha (Study on Fairness in Chinese Rural Land Distribution from a Gender Perspective – 1199 Nationwide Empirical Survey of Farmers and 2,450 Villages)', *Xian dai jing ji tan tao (Modern Economic Research)*, 10.

Zhou, J.L. (2001) 'Cheng zhen hua. Nong cun cheng shi hua. Cheng xiang yi ti hua – Conceptual Analysis of Urbanization', *Zhong guo nong cun jing ji (Chinese Rural Economy)*, 5.

Zhu, L. (2000) 'Nong di fen pei zhong de xing bie ping deng wen ti (Gender Inequality in China's Land Tenure System)', *Jing ji Yan jiu (Economic Research Journal)*, 9.

4

Concession in Stamp Duty: A Tool for Women Empowerment

An Empirical Assessment

SAROJ ARORA AND PREM SINGH

The concept of women's empowerment can be considered as a process as well as an outcome. The term 'empowerment' mainly deals with 'power' and 'being powerful' meaning a power that entails the process of change. In the context of Indian society, this means that deep rooted forms of inequality, built into traditional structure, are based on caste and gender, and they dis empower the lowest caste in the caste hierarchy and women. In this way, empowerment protects an individual from deprivation, manipulation and coercion (Beteille 1999). Economic empowerment can prevent one from insecurity, marginalization and deprivation.

Gender discrimination in property ownership is a worldwide phenomenon. Women constitute half of the world's population and produce between 60 to 80 per cent of the food in developing countries but they own less than 10 per cent of the world's property (United Nations 1980). They are frequently denied the right to own and inherit property. In practice, few women own productive resources, even fewer effectively control it. This has a direct bearing on their status and places them at disadvantaged situation in terms of securing a place to live and maintaining resources for their livelihood. Property right also needs to be understood as a fundamental human right.

Since the majority of women do not have adequate access to secure property rights, their realization remains an important issue from the socio-economic and political point of view. The absence or insecurity of property rights is a central and ubiquitous cause of poverty and gender inequalities in various societies (Sachs 2006). The gender-based discrimination in the accessibility and ownership of resources including productive resources such as land and other immovable assets was considered to be embedded in the social, legal, economic and political structures which further perpetuate inequalities in other spheres (Batliwala 1996). It is believed that these types of discriminatory practices can be removed only by enabling women to gain equal access to and control over these resources and by transforming institutions and structure through which the ideology and practice of subordination are reinforced.

Initiatives for Gender Equality in Context of Property Right

The United Nations Research Institute for Social Development mentions that there have been both considerable progresses through the 1990s in making formal laws pertaining to landed property more gender equitable as well as repeated failures in actually putting statutes to work (United Nations 2006). In many cases, developing countries have enacted laws and policies to provide women with greater rights to control and manage property. Many of these countries have amended constitutions or implemented registration to guarantee rights of women to inherit/transfer property on an equitable basis with men. However, it has been experienced that often barriers to the exercise of property rights are found to exist *de facto* as a result of poor enforcement of formal rights or of deeply embedded social norms. Therefore, enacting formal laws that provide women with property rights do not necessarily guarantee that they will be able to exercise their rights unless an enforcement mechanism is strengthened by making legal assistance and support services affordable or accessible for women (Izumi 2007). In many countries, formal statutory law operates in conjunction with customary law and cultural norms, and practices based on patriarchal attitudes make it difficult to enforce women's legal rights to land. Thus, the legal empowerment of women through property rights would require sustained efforts. For women, the existence of inheritance rules that call for male and female heirs to receive equal consideration in testamentary distributions are an important step on the path towards empowerment (Agarwal 1994).

Benefits if Women Own Property

Studies have shown that the existing gender inequality weakens women's bargaining capacity and place them at the receiving end which further weakens their decision-making powers in the household. Also, there is always a constant threat before women of being evicted out of the home in case of domestic violence. Lack of support system and institutional mechanism make women's condition more vulnerable (Government of Gujarat 2011). The problem is intertwined with that of inheritance, as many widows and daughters are evicted from land and property. Many formal or informal legal systems still favour men in distributions made by inheritance (Deere and Leon 2003). In the Indian society, one finds explicit gender bias in property ownership which stem from deep-rooted cultural distinctions such as caste and gender. The challenge then is to create conditions for property rights not just at the legal level, whether customary or formal that treats men and women differently but also through mechanisms that can fundamentally change mental framework and social practices at different levels of a society. Such an existing situation has drawn attention for changes in the policy and legal framework. Various corrective measures were introduced in India. For instance, the ninth five year (1997–2002) document included a section on *Gender and Land Rights* and emphasized the need for land ownership by women. Property related laws were reviewed and the Hindu Succession Act was amended. The new property law now entitles widows and daughters to inherit (UN-Habitat 2006).

According to the International Centre for Research on Women (2005) women who own property or otherwise control assets directly gain benefits not only as use of the land and getting higher incomes out of it but also get a secure place to live. Besides empowering women, property right does a great deal to alleviate poverty and reduce mal-nutrition, as women who earn more spend a higher proportion of their income to keep their children healthy and well fed. Providing women with the right to use, own and transfer immovable properties is also important to promote entrepreneurial activity and to provide women with a platform for building strong families and strong business. Property rights also bring increased economic benefits when linked to functional credit system and market (Deininger and Chamorro 2004). It is argued that although a majority of women may not be taxed currently as property owners, they will automatically become a more important part of the tax net and contribute in the country's economy once the country develops (Barnett and Grown 2004). Therefore, it is necessary to identify the building blocks of the property system, be it as a system of rules that defines the bundle of rights and obligations between people and assets; as a system of governance; as a functioning market for the exchange of assets or as an instrument of social policy. States can attempt to balance inequality and solidarity.

Initiative by Indian States

In India, the primary way of acquiring land by women is either through the family inheritance or through purchase. In order to empower women economically, some of the Indian states have initiated a Scheme of providing concession in duty including registration fee to women registering property in their name. The benefits of the Scheme are manifold. The programme is based on the basic premise that ownership of productive resources by women would make them socially, economically and legally secure. It will also help women in building their confidence and strive towards self-reliance, increase their power and ultimately result in their overall empowerment.

It was found that out of 28 states and 7 union territories in the country, 10 states and one union territory implemented the Scheme of concession in duty to women property buyers. These states are: Andhra Pradesh, Assam, Delhi, Gujarat, Haryana, Madhya Pradesh, Punjab, Rajasthan, Uttarakhand and Uttar Pradesh and the union territory of Puducherry. Delhi was one of the pioneering states which has implemented the Scheme in 2003, that is, during the tenth five year plan (2002–2007). Gradually, some other states and a union territory also revised and reduced duty in favour of women property buyers. For instance, Gujarat, Madhya Pradesh and Rajasthan have implemented the Scheme in 2004; Haryana in 2005; Uttar Pradesh and Uttarakhand in 2006, that is, during the tenth five year plan (2002–2007); Punjab, Andhra Pradesh and Puducherry in 2004 (amended in 2009); and Uttarakhand in 2009. Assam introduced this programme of late in 2008, that is, during eleventh five year plan (2007–2012). In Assam, there is a proposal for further slashing of the duty from 5 per cent to 2 per cent. There is also a proposal for slashing of registration fee for all irrespective of males or females. It is important to mention that there are states, such as Goa – known for its beaches, where although provision of concession in the duty to women property buyers has not been made yet, the current duty is as low as 2 per cent.

It has been experienced that the implementation of the Scheme by the states motivated a large number of families in registering property in women's name and there were exponential increase in the number of women beneficiaries. For instance, in Madhya Pradesh, 1,489,777 women got benefitted by the Scheme during the financial year 2004–2011. During 2008–2009, there was a record breaking 47.64 per cent documents registered in favour of women in comparison with the total number of documents registered during the same financial year (Inspector General, Registration, Madhya Pradesh 2011). In Uttarakhand 43,152 women benefitted from the Scheme during the financial year 2009–10 (Government of Uttaranchal 2006). In Gujarat, during 2004 to 2010, about 9,77,883 women have benefitted from the Scheme since the registration fee exemption came into force (Inspector General, Registration, Gujarat 2011). In Puducherry, 76,529 women benefitted between 2005–2011 financial years. Out of which 4,468 women sold the property within 5 years (2006–2011), after repaying the concession availed (Government of Puducherry 2011).

Objectives of the present paper are to assess the incremental increase in women's ownership of property after the introduction of the Scheme, women's role in decision-making with regard to the purchase of property, retention rate of property purchased in women's name and the impact of the Scheme towards empowering women. It also attempts to estimate the loss of revenue to the state exchequer due to the implementation of the Scheme. The study was conducted in the three districts namely Lucknow, Ghaziabad and Jaunpur in the state of Uttar Pradesh in India. Around 1,000 women beneficiaries of the Scheme were interviewed. Household data analysis reveals following results about women beneficiaries of the Scheme.

Implementation of the Scheme in the State of Uttar Pradesh

In Uttar Pradesh, for the first time, the Scheme of concession in the duty was allowed in respect of certain deeds executed in favour of women vide the notification dated 23 February 2006, that is, during tenth five year plan. With this, the existing notification no. K.S.V./5-3706-11-98-500 (20)-98 dated 31 August 1998 was amended. By the aforesaid notification, the rate of duty which was uniformly 8 per cent in respect of men and women was reduced to 6 per cent subject to certain conditions laid down in the said notification for a value of ₹ 10,00,000 in favour of one or more women individually or severally on certain instruments. If the property was valued more than ₹ 10,00,000, the duty was calculated as per the prevalent rate. Further, vide the notification dated 30 June 2008, the rate of duty in favour of women was further reduced. Due to the reduction, the current revised duty in the state is 4 per cent for woman vendor and 5 per cent for man vendor. The maximum limit of registration fee is ₹ 10,000. With the inception of the Scheme in the state, 25,36,543 women registered property in their name and benefitted during three financial years viz. 2008–2009, 2009–2010 and 2010–2011 (Inspector General, Registration, Uttar Pradesh 2011).

Socio-economic Profile of Women Beneficiaries of the Scheme

Caste category of women beneficiaries of the Scheme revealed that most of these women (57.70%) were from the General Caste followed by Other Backward Castes (32.50%) and Scheduled Castes (9.80%). Religion-wise data shows that 84.10 per cent belonged to Hindu religion, 10.60 per cent were Muslims, and few of them were Sikhs, Christians and Jains (4.10%, 1.10% and

0.10%, respectively). Age group of the respondents' shows that majority of 72 per cent were from productive age group of 36–60 years. About 88 per cent were married, 9.50 per cent were widows, 1.80 per cent were unmarried, 0.50 per cent were separated and 0.20 per cent were divorced. Educational status of the respondents shows that 38.50 per cent were graduates, 20.5 per cent were intermediate pass, 15.40 per cent were literate and 13.30 per cent were High School pass. Remaining 0.60 per cent had acquired a technical/professional degree. Out of the total, 11.70 per cent were illiterate. Occupational status shows that 80.8 per cent were house makers; 5.7 per cent were engaged in business and 5 per cent in private sector. A small percentage of 3.9 per cent were found working in the government sector and 3 per cent were having income out of rent/remittance/pension. A small number of them (1.6%) were found engaged in casual labour.

Purchasing Property in Women's Name

An analysis on the type of property purchased, purpose of purchasing property in women's name and sources of awareness about the Scheme of concession in duty to women property buyers are described below:

Most of the respondents reported purchasing residential plot or house (44.30 % and 43.50% respectively) while 8.80 per cent have reported purchasing agricultural land. Respondents reported purchasing flat and shop were lesser in number (1.70% each). Thus, less number of respondents had purchased productive assets. Number of women purchasing agricultural land was found higher in Jaunpur district. Type of property purchased and the occupational status were found interrelated to a great extent. Assets for residential purpose such as house, house plots and flats were the main assets purchased across all the occupational categories but respondents who were engaged in business sector preferred to purchase a shop.

Majority of the respondents (96.10%) said that they were aware of the amount spent in purchasing property while the remaining were not aware of the amount spent.

As far as purpose of purchasing property was concerned, in 77.70 per cent cases property was purchased for residential purpose and 9.10 per cent as asset for investment. Rest of them purchased property for income generation such as agriculture or business (8.40% and 4.50% respectively). A minuscule 0.30 per cent purchased property for other purposes. Thus, the main purposes of purchasing property were mainly house for residential purpose and in some cases for income generation and investment. It is important to mention that the respondents who have reported purchasing flat or shop, a sizeable number of them have told that their purpose was investment (See Table 1).

Table 1

For What Purpose the Property Was Purchased?

Districts	*Residential*	*Investment*	*Agriculture*	*Business*	*Others*	*Total*
Lucknow	704 (79.10)	85 (9.55)	57 (6.40)	41 (4.61)	3 (0.34)	890 (100)
Ghaziabad	55 (91.67)	1 (1.67)	0 (0.00)	4 (6.67)	0 (0.00)	60 (100)
Jaunpur	18 (36.00)	5 (10.00)	27 (54.00)	0 (0.00)	0 (0.00)	50 (100)
Total	777 (77.70)	91 (9.10)	84 (8.40)	45 (4.50)	3 (0.30)	1,000 (100)

Source: Household survey. Percentage in brackets.

It was found that both informal channels such as friends/relatives, formal channel such as Housing Board or semi-formal agencies such as property dealers and real estate developers and advertising agencies were the main sources from where the property was purchased. Data revealed that 34.40 per cent respondents purchased property from relatives/friends, 27.90 per cent from Housing Board and 19.70 per cent from the property dealers. About 14.70 per cent respondents have purchased property through advertisements and 0.80 per cent bought it from real estate developers. Around 2.50 per cent respondents reported purchasing from other sources.

In order to find out about the level of awareness related to the concession in duty to women property buyers, women beneficiaries of the Scheme were asked whether they were aware of any such Scheme. Out of total respondents, 33.20 per cent were aware of the Scheme, 8.90 per cent were found partially aware but 57.90 per cent were found unaware. An analysis across three sample districts shows that awareness about the Scheme was higher in Ghaziabad and Lucknow, which are relatively advanced compared to Jaunpur. Notably, awareness, educational level and the occupational status of the respondents were found interrelated to a great extent. Higher the educational level, greater was the awareness about the Scheme. Similarly, the respondents engaged in formal or semi-formal sector and earning income were found more aware as compared to the house makers.

The major sources of information about the Scheme were family members (61.09%), followed by neighbours/friends (13.68%), advertisement (13.07%), deed writers (6.99%) and government officials (5.17%). Few came to know through other sources.

Women Beneficiaries of the Scheme and their Role in Decision-Making Process

An analysis of respondent's relationship with the person who played an important role in decision-making to purchase property in women's name shows that it has been mostly husbands who took decision (66.90%), while 15.70 per cent said that they themselves decided and 15.20 per cent said that their family members decided. A small number of them (2.20%) informed that the decision was taken by others. District-wise analysis shows that the number of cases where respondents themselves decided were higher in Ghaziabad whereas husband and family members were found playing important role in Jaunpur and Lucknow (See Table 2). A person who decided that the property should be purchased in women's name and type of property purchased were found interrelated to some extent. Husbands and family members were found playing an important role when productive assets (agricultural land or shop) were purchased. But when flat for residential purpose was purchased, respondents themselves also played an important role.

Similarly, on the question whether respondents were involved in negotiating the deal, 30.80 per cent respondents have told that they were involved in negotiating the deal; however, large number of them (69.20%) said that they were not involved.

Table 2

Who Decided the Property Should be Purchased in Your Name?

District	*Husband*	*Self*	*Family Member*	*Others*	*Total*
Lucknow	599 (67.30)	131 (14.72)	140 (15.73)	20 (2.25)	890 (100)
Ghaziabad	30 (50.00)	25 (41.67)	5 (8.33)	0 (0.00)	60 (100)
Jaunpur	40 (80.00)	1 (2.00)	7 (14.00)	2 (4.00)	50 100)
Total	669 (66.90)	157 (15.70)	152 (15.20)	22 (2.20)	1,000 (100)

Source: Household survey. Percentage in brackets.

On being questioned whether the property would have been purchased in their name had this concession not been there, a small number of the respondents (4.80%) said they would have purchased property even if concession would not have been there. About 45.70 per cent said that they would not have while 49.50 per cent were found indecisive and did not comment.

Financial Sources for Purchasing the Property

Since most of the women beneficiaries of the Scheme were home makers, hence it was found pertinent to study the sources of finance for purchasing property. It was found that funds were contributed mainly through four sources viz. down payment, savings, loan and other sources. Multiple responses have been received. Data analysis has shown that out of the total sample population, 90.3 per cent reported contributing through down payment, 13.8 per cent respondents contributed through savings and 21.5 per cent respondents reported taking loan. Out of total respondents reported taking loan, 30.70 per cent respondents reported taking loan by themselves. And remaining 69.30 per cent of them have told that their family members (husband or father) took loan. Loan was taken either from public or private sector banks and remaining have lent from cooperative banks, housing finance companies or family members. Caste-wise analysis revealed that most of these respondents belonged to the General Caste. Lesser number of OBCs or SCs reported taking loan. About 13 per cent respondents reported that they arranged funds through other sources.

Amount contributed through various sources ranges between ₹ 1 to ₹ 10 lakh. For instance, amount contributed through down payment was in the range of ₹ 1 lakh to more than ₹ 9 lakh. Contribution through savings was found in the range of ₹ 1–10 lakh and contribution made through loan and other sources were found in the range of ₹ 1 lakh to more than ₹ 10 lakh. Most of these respondents reported taking loan in the range of ₹ 2.5–5 lakh. The interest rate charged on loan varies between 5–15 per cent. Duration of loan repayment varies between 1 to 20 years. Out of total respondents who reported taking loan, 37.88 per cent of them admitted facing problems in taking loan. About 44 per cent said that the processing of loan application took a long time and around 24 per cent said that the procedure involved in releasing loan was complicated and lengthy. About 16 per cent of them told that the cost of property was higher than the loan amount sanctioned by the bank. About 12 per cent said that they paid commission to the middlemen which was an additional financial burden on them while the remaining 4 per cent have told that the interest rate charged on loan was very high.

Following case study shows how accessibility of loan becomes inaccessible to poor and illiterate women:

> S. Nishad is a 32-year-old married housewife, living in Nishatganj colony who has some basic education. Her husband works as a mason. She purchased a residential plot for which she managed money partly out of family savings and partly took loan from her mother. Her husband also took loan from his friends. Later on, she sold the plot as it was located far-off. She was not aware of the concession in the duty for women but when she went to the registry office; her husband and she came to know about the Scheme through a middleman.
>
> S. Nishad showed her helplessness and anger for not being able to take loan from the formal financial institutions particularly banks. She said that since they are poor and illiterate, hence, banking facility is not accessible to them. 'Banking procedures are very complicated and cumbersome. Bank officials do not treat us nicely as we are poor and illiterate'. She rather posed a question before the interviewer that from where a poor person who has no regular income can provide documents such as income tax return and guarantors which are the prerequisite for getting loan?

For expanding access to credit for the people particularly the poor marginalized communites, the government has made provision in which both tangible and intangible property can be used legally as collateral to secure a loan. In the present study, it was found that out of the total respondents who reported taking loan by themselves, majority of them (94.64%) have said that collateral was not required for taking loan and remaining 5.36 per cent have told that collateral was required. Most of these respondents who have reported taking loan by themselves have taken loan from their family members or friends. Regarding loan repayment, most of the respondents (47.83%) reported that the loan was repaid by their husbands, 43.48 per cent respondents said that loan was repaid out of self-earned income, 6.52 per cent were repaying out of income earned from their property and 2.17 per cent informed that their parents were repaying the loan.

On the question of their individual contribution in purchasing property, it was found to range between ₹ 1 lakh to ₹ 10 lakh. Although majority of them reported contributing either up to ₹ 2.5 lakh (51.11%) or in the range of ₹ 2.5–5 lakh (28.15%). Only 0.74 per cent reported contributing in the range of ₹ 5–7.5 lakh. Individual's contribution for purchasing property was found higher in Lucknow as compared to Ghaziabad and Jaunpur districts.

Retention Rate of the Property Purchased in Women's Name

Sustainability of the concession in duty to women property buyers depends on various factors such as the property purchased is not sold or not for speculation purposes or not transferred on power of attorney (PoA) basis. Rather it was purchased to strengthen women position.

Household data shows that in 98.90 per cent cases the property purchased in the name of the women was not sold while 1.10 per cent informed that the property purchased in their name has already been sold. Reasons for selling the property were – due to distress or to get profit (45.45% each) whereas 9.09 per cent did not want to share the reason. District-wise analysis shows that in Lucknow district, property was sold mainly due to distress situations whereas cases of selling property to earn profit were more in Ghaziabad. Following case exhibits an example of distress sale:

> Seema Gupta, a 52-year-old educated woman lives in Lucknow. Her husband runs a medical shop. Seema purchased a house plot in her name and constructed a beautiful house. She did not have enough money, hence took loan from State Bank of India.
>
> Due to financial loss in business and family disputes, she could not repay the bank loan timely. Bank officials started visiting her house every now and then. Sometime they used to insult them for not paying equated monthly installment (EMI). To avoid humiliation due to her inability to pay the EMI to the bank, she along with her husband decided to sell the house. They are now living in a rented house.

Respondents who reported selling of property were asked whether their consent was taken prior to the sale of property. Majority of the respondents (90.91%) told that their consent was taken prior to the sale of property whereas 9.09 per cent informed that their consent was not taken. District-wise data analysis shows that the cases of not taking consent were found in Lucknow.

Respondents were further asked whether they could dispose off the property without taking consent of other family members to which 31.70 per cent said that they could dispose of property without taking consent of anyone in the family and remaining 68.30 per cent said that they could not. District-wise analysis shows that the number of respondents reporting that they could dispose of the property without taking anyone's consent was larger in Lucknow followed by Ghaziabad and Jaunpur.

Household data analysis revealed that out of the total sample population, 18.10 per cent reported that the property purchased in their name was transferred to some other family members on PoA basis. In majority of the cases (97.80%) it was transferred to a male family member. Only in a small number of cases (2.20%) it was transferred to a female family member. Thus, despite imposing ban on PoA such cases were found taking place. The Honourable Supreme Court of India has banned transfer of property through PoA as such transactions cause loss of revenue and increased litigation. The bench said, 'in the absence of a deed of conveyance (duly stamped and registered as required by law), no right, title or interest in an immovable property can be transferred' (Singh 2011). It pronounced that any contract of sale which was not registered as sale deed would fall short of the requirements of the relevant provisions for the Transfer of Property Act and could not confer any title.

Impact of the Scheme in the Empowerment of Women

Impact of the Scheme in the empowerment of women was assessed on 15 parameters viz. (1) Income generation/savings from property; (2) Feel economically secured and confident; (3) Able to deal with bank/government officials; (4) Can take decisions related to purchase; (5) Satisfaction that children would inherit the property; (6) Able to get acceptance/respect in the family; (7) Views are given more importance while taking decision related to children's education, health and marriage; (8) Increase in self-respect/esteem; (9) Neighbours/friends started respecting more than earlier; (10) Started participating in various informal/social associations; (11) Confidence in interacting with others; (12) Able to influence the decision about the number of children they would like to have (only if applicable); (13) Able to get access to health services independently; (14) Decline in domestic violence; and (15) Feel secured of not being evicted/disowned. Responses of 1,000 respondents on these 15 parameters were summarized which was on 5 point scale of 'completely agree', 'partially agree', 'no difference', 'partially disagree' and 'completely disagree'.

Data analysis has shown that respondents found significant changes on six parameters after owning property in their name. These aspects were: (1) Feel economically secured and confident; (2) Satisfaction that children would inherit the property; (3) Able to get acceptance/respect in the family; (4) Views are given more importance while taking decision related to children's education, health and marriage; (5) Confidence in interacting with others; and (6) Able to get access to health services independently. Notably, overwhelming response was found on the issue where women beneficiaries felt satisfied that their children would inherit the property. It shows that asset building was not only the economic security in the present, but was perceived for the better future of the next generation also.

The following case corroborates how women perceive property ownership as empowering not only them but also their children:

> Mrs Parvati, a 35-year-old woman is working in a private nursing home. Earlier she was living in a rented house. Her husband runs a small sweet shop. Unfortunately, two years ago her husband fell sick and there was a serious financial crisis in the family. She felt that if something happened to her husband, she and her children would become shelter less. She shared her problems with some of her colleagues who informed about the Scheme of concession in the duty for women property buyers. She contacted a property dealer and purchased a residential plot costing ₹ 2 lakh. She managed funds out of the family savings and took financial help from her mother's side and constructed a house. She stated, 'Now I feel self-confident to think that nobody can evict us from my house. I also feel good when I think that this property will be transferred to my children and they will have safe future'.

On another four parameters, respondents found moderate changes after owning property in their name. These parameters were: (1) Able to deal with bank/government officials; (2) Can take decisions related to purchase; (3) Increase in self-respect/esteem; and (4) Feel secured of not being evicted/disowned. The case of Farzana reveals how property ownership enhanced her sense of security that nobody can evict her now.

> Mrs Farzana, an illiterate, married Muslim woman belongs to a Ghosi community. She lives in Vrindavan Colony in a joint family. Earlier she was residing in an unregistered slum but she was evicted and became shelter less. She did not have the money to buy a new house so she sold her jewellery and arranged money to purchase a small house on subsidy basis. She has to pay the amount in 10 annual installments. She has already paid the premium in three installments amounting to ₹ 11,000 each. But due to poor economic conditions and no regular source of income, she is facing difficulties in paying the remaining installments. She is too poor to deal with the bank and also unless she pays the remaining amount, she is not entitled to get loan on the present house. But she feels confident as the house is in her name and now nobody can evict her.

On the remaining five parameters where respondents found less impact of the Scheme were: (1) Income generation/savings from property; (2) Neighbours/friends started respecting more than earlier; (3) Started participating in various informal/social associations; (4) Able to influence the decision about the number of children they would like to have (only if applicable); and (5) Decline in domestic violence.

It was found that 54.10 per cent respondents found that their economic condition has become better after owning property in their name. About 43.90 per cent have found no change and 2.0 per cent of them have said that they have become poorer.

Women Beneficiaries and Revenue Loss Due to the Implementation of the Scheme

Duty and registration fee are the second major sources of revenue after sales tax in Uttar Pradesh (www.registryoffice.up.nic.in). The revenue forgone in the state due to concession in the duty during the financial year 2008–2009 was ₹ 4,37,76,06,622 out of which the total revenue loss in three sample districts was ₹ 69,20,24,000 (Inspector General, Registration, Uttar Pradesh 2011). Three districts where maximum number of women got benefitted in the state during 2008–09 were Aligarh, Ghaziabad and Lucknow. Contrary to it, during the same financial year, three districts where less number of women benefitted by the Scheme were Kausambi, Mahoba and Mahamayanagar. The latter three districts are less developed compared to the former three districts. Out of three districts where documents registered in favour of women were the highest was Aligarh; 42.16 per cent out of the total documents got registered in Aligarh district alone followed by Ghaziabad and Lucknow.

Major Findings and Recommendations

1. Findings of the household surveys show that the concession in duty has motivated a large number of women in purchasing property in their name. Most of the respondents admitted that they would not purchase property had this concession not been there.

2. Findings have also shown that the property ownership brought significant changes in their lives on the following parameters: (i) Feel economically secured and confident; (ii) Satisfaction that children would inherit property; (iii) Able to get acceptance/respect in the family; (iv) Views are given more importance while taking decision related to children's education, health and marriage; (v) Confidence in interacting with others; and (vi) Able to get access to health services independently.
3. However, there were few pitfalls also in the programme. For instance, despite the fact that the large number of women in the state of Uttar Pradesh benefitted by the concession in the stamp duty, awareness about the Scheme was found among less number of beneficiaries. There is a need to create awareness about the Scheme among women with greater emphasis on marginal communities so that they could be brought in the ambit of the programme and avail benefit. Awareness can be generated through formal as well as informal channels.

   Accessibility of loan to women property buyers emerged as one of the major issue. Women found it difficult to approach formal financial institutions. Many of the respondents who approached banking institutions for loan encountered problems such as complicated procedure, delay in processing the loan application or expectation of bribe by the middlemen. Examples of generating funds through SHGs (although only in rare cases) have come across. There is a need for simplifying banking procedure and making provision of soft loan on low interest rate particularly for women of poor families.
4. Women should be encouraged to become SHGs member to meet out savings and credit needs to purchase property in their name.
5. The retention rate of property transferred in women's name was found very high. Emphasis should be made not to sell the property at least for minimum of 10–12 years.
6. Registration and mutation are two separate departments which work independent to each other. It was observed that although large number of women got property

registered in their name yet most of them did not get that mutated. In the absence of mutation, women's rights are poorly protected and they may lose the asset. Women usually avoid mutation for various reasons such as lack of knowledge, complicated and time consuming process and limited access to information.

Women should be encouraged to mutate their registered property. Registration and mutation of property documents are inter-linked, hence need to be merged along with other associated departments and bring them under one ministry. Jawaharlal Nehru National Urban Renewal Mission (JNNURM) recommended bringing these two departments under one Ministry but so far no action has been taken in this direction.

7. Land administration functions are dispersed among many agencies such as Sub Registrar Office, Survey Settlement, Land Revenue, Municipal Corporation, Housing Board and Housing Development Authority. Although these agencies are interdependent yet work separately which causes inconveniences to women. Even though the responsibilities are well defined, but in practice this creates confusion among users, prevents realization of economies of scale and increases the cost of providing land administration services to the detriment of the poor including women. This also leads to overlapping competencies and pave way for non-transparent practices. Experience worldwide shows that delays in tenure in security due to rivalries and conflicting interests are inevitable when a number of competing agencies are simultaneously responsible for the implementation of property rights.

8. Large numbers of houses are constructed by private developers/colonizers. The state can foster the social fabric through property rights, such as in housing and neighbourhood development, low interest loans and the low priced sale of state land.

   There can be a provision of certain percentage of the land reserved for housing particularly for low income group women. Although such provisions are there but these are in bits and pieces and not mandatory. Hence these are very often manipulated by the resourceful people. A similar provision was made by the state of Madhya Pradesh. Madhya Pradesh government enacted as part of the Colonizers' Act requires 15 per cent of the land to be reserved for construction of houses for the shelter less or payment of a sum equivalent to the officially determined price of the land to be reserved. The policy has made land available for housing to more than 6,000 poor households in central city locations in Bhopal alone and substantial funds for land procurement and development (Banerjee and Iyer 2005).

9. Apparently, the provision of concessions in duty is causing revenue loss to the state exchequer. But proponents of this Scheme argue that its purpose is to empower women by making them owner of productive resources. Hence, it is worthwhile to continue with such provisions at least for the time being. It is said that the revenue loss due to prevailing provision is temporary and the outcomes are far reaching. It is also said that although majority of women may not be taxed currently as property owners, as countries develop and as women acquire property rights in housing and land, they will automatically become a more important part of the tax net and contribute in the country's economy.
10. Around one-tenth of the respondents have reported that the property purchased in their name was transferred to some other family members on PoA basis. It is important to mention that if property is owned on PoA basis, a person can neither sell that property nor take loan from the bank. In other words, the owner of property cannot exercise his/her absolute power in its use or disposal.
    Property purchased in women's name should not be allowed to be transferred in someone else's name on PoA basis. In case, it becomes necessary, a provision of compulsory registration of PoA should be made.
11. The locations of the agency dealing with the registration and mutation of landed property should be as decentralized as possible and easily accessible to women and poor who are unable to bear the costs of travelling long distances in order to register or transfer property.

Modern technology can help to improve transparency and at the same time make administration more accessible (Lobo and Balakrishnan 2002). In Uttar Pradesh, where computerization of registry started in 2009 there is a need to streamline the entire backlog of registry documents.

12. Property dealers and land mafia have nexus with politicians and they sometime misuse the provisions of the Scheme implemented for the benefit of women. There is a need to evolve a proper check and balance mechanism to curb such practices.

Acknowledgement

The authors acknowledge the immense help extended to them by Mr Alok Kumar, IAS, former Inspector General, Stamp and Registration, Uttar Pradesh and Mr P.K. Pandey, IAS, present Inspector General, Stamp and Registration, Uttar Pradesh for providing the data. Special thanks are due to Mrs Rina Singh for facilitating during the fieldwork.

REFERENCES

Agarwal, B. (1994) *A Field of One's Own: Gender and Land Rights in South Asia*. Cambridge: Cambridge University Press.

Banerjee, A. and L. Iyer (2005) 'History, Institutions, and Economic Performance: The Legacy of Colonial Land Tenure Systems in India', *The American Economic Review*, 95 (4).

Barnett, K. and C. Grown (2004) *Gender Impacts of Government Revenue Collection: The Case of Taxation*, Commonwealth Economic Paper Series. London: Economic Affairs Division of the Commonwealth Secretariat.

Batliwala, S. (1996) 'Empowering Women: South Asian Framework', *Seminar*, 88–91.

Beteille, A. (1999) 'Empowerment', *Economic and Political Weekly*, 34 (10–11), 6–13 March.

Cheneval, F. (2008) Empowering the Poor through Property Rights. In M. Albright, H. De Soto and N. Singh (Eds), *Making the Law Work for Everyone*. Vol. II, New York: Post Print.

Deere, C. Diana and M. Leon (2003) 'The Gender Asset Gap: Land in Latin America', *World Development*, 31 (6).

Deininger, K. and J. Chamorro (2004) 'Investment and Equity Effects of Land Regularization: The Case of Nicargua', *Agricultural Economics*, 30 (2).

Government of Goa (2011) Law Department, Secretariat, Goa Letter No. 15-2011-LD (Estt)/11. Unpublished Government Communication, 11 July.

Government of Gujarat (2011) Exemption from the Registration Fee for Women. Department of Women and Child Development. Unpublished Government Communication.

Government of Puducherry (2011) Special Secretary, Department of Revenue and Disaster Management, Letter No. 1/Misc/Rev/C.3/2011 (Vol. VI). Unpublished Government Communication, 29 June.

Government of Uttaranchal (2006) Uttaranchal, Finance Section–9, No. 299/XXVII (9)/2006. Dehradun: Government Gazette, 18 August.

Inspector General, Registration, Madhya Pradesh (2011) Letter No. 2140/Ka/2011, Registration Bhawan in front of old Vidhan Sabha. Bhopal: Madhya Pradesh Government Press, 6 August.

Inspector General, Registration, Uttar Pradesh (2011) Letter No. 4872/stamp/vividh-59. Allahabad: Uttar Pradesh Government Press, 26 April.

International Centre for Research on Women (2005) *Property Ownership for Women Enriches, Empowers and Protects: Towards Achieving the Third Millennium Development Goal to Promote Gender Equality and Empower Women*. Washington, DC: International Centre for Research on Women.

Izumi, Kaori (2007) 'Gender Based Violence and Property Grabbing in Africa: A Denial of Women's Liberty and Security', *Gender and Development*, 15 (1).

Lobo, A. and S. Balakrishnan (2002) *Report on Service of Bhoomi Kiosks: An Assessment of Benefits by Users of the Computerised Land Records System in Karnataka*. Bangalore: Public Affairs Centre.

Sachs, J. (2006) *The End of Poverty: Economic Possibilities of Our Time*. New York: Penguin.

Singh, G. (2011) 'No Property Sale on Power of Attorney: Supreme Court', *Mail Today*, New Delhi Edition, October 13.

UN-Habitat (2006) Progress Report on 'Removing Discrimination Against Women in Respect of Property and Inheritance Rights'. Nairobi: United Nations.

United Nations (1980) *Report of the World Conference of the United Nations Decade for Women: Equality, Development and Peace*. Doc A/Cof. 94/35.

United Nations (2006) *Land Tenure Reform and Gender Equality*. Geneva: United Nations Research Institute for Social Development.

www.registryoffice.up.nic.in (Retrieved on 3 September 2013).

5

Hand Embroidery as a Tool of Empowering Rural Women of Punjab

ANU H. GUPTA AND SHALINA MEHTA

Punjab, the land of five rivers, has villages as integral units in the state structure and family as an important entity in the village. The family organization is strictly patriarchal. The eldest male of the house is the head of family and he is the one who makes all decisions for the family whether it is related to economic matters or social matters or even education of their children. Noopur (1989) mentions Margret Mead's cross-cultural analysis of sex roles suggesting that regardless of specific tasks, male control of prestige defines the male task as more important.

The women's place or status has been restricted to the performance of domestic chores fulfilling the role of a dutiful wife and mother. They are expected to be obedient, respecting their husbands and clan members and submissive. Married women have to observe more number of restrictions as compared to the unmarried ones. They have a greater range of responsibilities and their life revolves around cooking meals, cleaning the house, taking care of children, sick, elderly other family members as well as animals. Noopur (1989) mentions various roles of women in the family organization as a daughter, a wife and a mother. Punjabi women believe that it is their duty to perform household chores to their best. Girls grow up listening to statements such as – '*when you will be married, you will be expected to do all household work perfectly and if you don't do, you cannot come up to the expectations of your in-laws, they will blame us for not teaching you anything*'. Hence the girls place a great importance on the house work and hence develop the habit of doing these chores in earnestness. Many women are also partially engaged in agricultural activities. They are first to rise, before the crack of dawn and start the day's work. Their daily life is a juggling act as they try to fit in a vast range of tasks and responsibilities. Mitra (1997) feels women were conditioned to sacrifice their own goals and ambitions, deny themselves their legitimate space and surrender any resources which might have contributed to their independence. They were always told to adjust, accept, accommodate and be dependent on men for support.

They are hardworking and dutiful towards their husbands. At the same time they are involved in creative process of decorating their house with beautiful *durries* (flat woven rugs), embroidered items, fabric painted products, knitted products etc. Embroidery is considered as an essential accomplishment of the woman since ancient time. She laughed and wept with the needle and the thread. Embroidery has for centuries been part of education of every well brought up Punjabi girl (Brijbhushan 1990). By embroidery women enriched their own lives and that of the family by creating objects of everyday use in home (Dhamija 2004).

In their leisure hour's mothers and grandmothers, the young and old, friends and relatives used to gather in the courtyard of someone's house to have sessions plying the *charkhas* (spinning wheel) and embroidering *phulkaris* (embroidered sheets/*odhinis* from Punjab). Gossiping, singing and laughing would come naturally while embroidering. They discussed and shared their experiences regarding methods and materials used as well as designs and pattern for the product they develop. The caring, sharing exchange of ideas and close interaction forms the very basis of social integration and makes an important statement through the stitches created by the needle and thread (Singh 2010). This is also the expression of cohesiveness (Gupta 2010).

In today's time too, after completing their regular routine household work, they sit together and create a variety of products. This is a relaxing activity for them as they are able to share their joys and sorrows with each other and also achieve a sense of pride in constructing beautiful products of daily use. Though village life is changing in terms of its culture but many things in the villages are same for women especially when it comes to money to be given to her, she is always pushed aside saying '*married women should not be given any money, otherwise she will do whatever she feels like...we will lose control over her*'. Mitra (1997) states the most basic factor which inhibited women from taking to entrepreneurship till recently was the attitude of society towards a women's role and place in the society.

Sharma (2012) illustrates rural women in India to be relatively powerless with no control over resources and have little decision-making power and often the decisions are imposed on them. The prevailing patriarchal ideologies which demand submission, sacrifice and silent suffering often undermines their capacity and deprives them of their share of resources. She adds that early marriage, lack of education, lack of economic independence, social customs and traditions are some of the reasons for women to lag behind. Sahay (1998) confirms continued inequality and vulnerability of women in all sectors – economic, social, political, education, health care, nutrition and legal. As women are oppressed in all spheres of life, they need to be empowered in all walks of life.

Empowering the women is important as this will bring a great change in her status in the family. With this improvement, she will never think herself to be nothing, she will never curse the creator on being a woman and she will never think that she is lagging behind. Nayak (1999) asserts that a woman must always remember that she is not only a reproductive being, but a productive individual and can greatly contribute to the advancement of society. Now-a-days women, may be in a small number, are coming forward to take up jobs at home like *pakhi* (hand fan) making, pickle making or other skills that they learn and exercise throughout their lives and embroidery is one of them which is practised to a great extent. Women are using this skill to earn. They are also creating self-help groups, sometimes with the help of Non-Government Organizations (NGOs) or societies which guide them to become independent and empower them. This gives them a sense of pride and confidence. Randhawa and Mann (2005) establish *Khes* (traditional thick cotton cloth used as a spread or blanket) making, embroidery, knitting and tailoring as preferred income generating activities amongst Punjabi women. The present paper explores some of the voices of such females where embroidery has helped them in many ways.

Concept of Empowerment

The World Bank (2013) describes empowerment as a process of increasing the capacity of individuals or groups to make choices and to transform those choices into desired actions and outcomes.

Pillai (1995) mentions it as an active, multi-dimensional procedure enabling women to realize their full identity and powers in all spheres of life. Sahay (1998) refers to empowerment as a process of awareness and capacity building leading to greater participation, to greater decision-making power and control, and to transformative action. Devasia and Devasia (1994) feels empowering of women involves a drastic, forceful and autonomous change in the sensitivity of expectation from women in our society. To help women to attain economic independence is the first priority for such a change.

Theoretical Premise

Embroidery contributes to the economic empowerment of women. Al-Kharouf (2010) shedding light on the experiences of women working in the field of embroidery reveals that embroidery learnt by women in the city of Amman as a hobby became a trade driven by economy, or a leisure activity or a way to prove oneself. Increase in income and self-esteem was an outcome of this profession. Embroidery is a tool for self-employment for women. Al-Dajani and Marlow (2010) also identify women's self-employment as a tool to assist in alleviating poverty and empowering individual women. Raheim and Bolden (1995) compare the potential for self-employment to facilitate women's economic empowerment with traditional options for women's economic self-sufficiency.

Embroidery is also considered as an identity for many women. It is recognized by several scholars as an instrument for constructing identity (Emeneau 1937). This is true not only for Toda women as stated by Emeneau but for every other section of gendered population engaged in this art form. Riley (2008) extends the argument and says textile making develops self-awareness and emits a sense of individual and cultural identity. Hall (1990) in identity empowerment theory suggests that women's understanding of the strengths and weakness of their personal and collective past and present will increase their sense of purpose and direction for the future. Through examination of their values, women become more able to consciously determine lifetime goals in their own interests.

The inextricable link between embroidery as an occupation, and the shaping of identity and role played by it in creating personal histories and achievements is explored by several scholars (Christiansen 1999; Laliberte-Rudman 2002; Reynolds 2003; Unruh 2004; Warin and Dennis 2005; Boerema, Russell and Aguilar 2010). Gale and Kaur (2002) connect craft people's personal identities to their practice as they express a commitment to their work and strongly identify with what they do and the way they feel about it. Ability to translate a leisure activity into a commercial venture gives a sense of control to women who have the courage to take it beyond the territorial boundaries of domesticity.

Embroidery as a collaborative effort helps in capacity building in different facets of life. Dol and Odame (2013) experienced that women working in a handicraft cooperative in Uganda were not only feeling empowered at the personal, collective and relational levels but also gained capacity in terms of the development of skills related to handicraft production, English and working with other individuals in a decision-making role. Women in villages jointly work in groups for income generation. Randhawa and Mann (2005) suggest that future focus of the self-help groups must be on capacity building and skill up-gradation of rural women. Islam (2011) argues that self-earning activities can empower rural women to enjoy their ability to reshape their lives. Moyle, Dollard and Biswas (2006) confirm collective efficacy, proactive attitude, self-esteem and self-efficacy; positive appraisals of self-worth, purpose and independence amongst women participating in self-help groups. Datta (2003) discussing the case of women working in Self Employed Women's Association (SEWA) argues that those who are active in the organization gain a new sense of empowerment that comes through active participation in decision-making and leadership. The skills they learn enable them to exude a sense of confidence in their families and communities as well.

The Subversive Stitch: Embroidery and the Making of the Feminine by Parker (1984) provides an anecdotal account of how embroidery was one of the central tasks expected of women in the 18th and 19th centuries. She argues that it was an outlet to express feelings of dismay and dislike. Embroidery was considered 'subversive' because in a patriarchal society it was supposed to provide pleasure and endow power on women. In most societies women invariably embroidered in groups, it became a medium for circulating femininity and for negotiating constraints of femininity. Women around the world pursue traditional crafts, and improvise, adapting their crafts to the context and the available materials (Edwards 2006).

This study explores the association of embroidery with the economic gains of the artisans. It also probes into aspects like identity formation, creative usage of time, feeling of accomplishment and a collective or collaborative venture through embroidery.

Methodology

The research is based on primary data collection from various villages surrounding Patiala district of Punjab. The data generation was made with the help of qualitative methods. In case of embroidery in Punjab, women are involved at various levels: artisan (those who embroider), middle agent/middle woman (who gets work from the shopkeepers and provide the same to the artisan and after completion of work, embroidered article is supplied back to the shopkeeper), members of self-help groups and the directors of NGOs. In-depth interviews with the artisans, middle agents, shopkeepers/retailers and NGOs, were undertaken. Homes of various artisans were visited where they were not only interviewed but also their working was captured. Focused group discussions, observations, narratives were some of the tools used to gather data.

Organizations which are working towards the women empowerment like National Bank for Agriculture and Rural

Development (NABARD) and offices of many NGOs and societies were a part of data collection where the directors or head/main members were interacted with. One of the fairs held in Chandigarh organized by Confederation of Indian Industry (CII) was also a source of information.

Embroidery as an Income Generating Activity

Embroidery is a source of economic support to the women artisan. Most of the artisans knew the art of embroidery from their young days and many have learnt or polished it after marriage. Artisans reported that they had prepared embroidered articles for their trousseau (clothing and other items that a bride and her family assemble for her marriage). The activity of embroidery is now undertaken as a profession by various artisans and middle women of Punjab for varied reasons. Women reported that they have interest in embroidery and this interest is pursued by them for economic reasons. They are able to earn something as well as save. Women engaged in this profession spend their earnings either on children or on household requirements and in few cases on themselves. They feel nice about the income generated by this activity because it gives them some amount of self-confidence.

An artisan from Samana Mandi, in Patiala district, though earns very less – ₹ 100 per month, still she says '*aapne hath ch paise rakhde han, jedi cheese di jarurat hoi, lai li*' (one should have money in her hand so that she can spend it whenever there is need, whatever she wants to spend it on). Some respondents believe that embroidery gives them a feeling of achievement that they can also do something. Another artisan from Gajjukheda village mentions her earning as a great help and says '*hamara hath thoda sa sokha ho jata hai*' (we are able to spend easily).

Stressing the importance of embroidery in her life one artisan said '*je mainu aanda hai tan hi main kaman rahi han*' (I am able to earn only because I know this embroidery). An artisan from Darukutia village, Patiala, said, 'We do embroidery throughout the day, we have only this work. We work for money. There is scarcity of money in our homes that is why we work. Our husbands never tell us to work, but the day to day expenditures are high, what can we do? We have to work'. One of the artisan at a village Gajjukheda remarked that both husband and wife should be earning in today's time. If a lady is literate, earning and self-dependent, she gets due regard at her home too. Embroidery helps these women artisans to have economic gains and independence with respect to their expenditure.

Embroidery as an Identity and Confidence Builder

One of my respondents was the Director of The Patiala Handloom Handicraft Workshop Cooperative Industrial Society Ltd. During the interview, she informed that she formed this society in 1995 for empowering the rural women where they were to be trained in embroidery and *phulkari* making. The motto which was spread among women was 'learn while earn'. Initially the villages were identified with respect to the specialty of the work – some villages were famous for embroidery with french knots, some for embroidery without blocking etc. Organizations like NABARD, Khadi and Village Industries Commission (KVIC), Small Industries Development Bank of India (SIDBI) were approached for various schemes and funding for training rural women in variety of courses, mainly embroidery, which could help them to earn. After training, these women were provided with the work either through personal contacts or through selling of embroidered articles in various fairs. They could also take orders from shopkeepers (especially from Patiala). She said that these activities build confidence in the artisan that she can also do something and gives sense of identity to these women. We understand that identity formation is a complex process. Women are often subjugated in their natal families as also in families of procreation. Years of suppression often scars their personalities and getting some work and financial independence is not necessarily the sole factor to give them a sense of personal identity.

The narratives cited above confirms the argument that textile making in the form of embroidery or produced with a different technique creates a sense of achievement amongst craft person (Emeneau 1937; Riley 2008). In fact Director of The Patiala Handloom Handicraft Workshop Cooperative Industrial Society Ltd. quoted her own example, 'I am now identified not only with my husband's name but my own name which is associated with phulkari embroidery, its revival in the state, upliftment of this traditional craft and the women associated (artisans)'. She has a cluster and a facility centre in the village Thus, in Patiala district. Women of varied age groups come here to learn embroidery. Health camps are also organized for these women where they are educated about their health issues. Hence such trainings create more awareness, build confidence and self-esteem amongst the participating women. Menon (1998) confirms that training, educating women, orienting them towards technical issues raises women's self-esteem and enables these women to determine what they wish to do with their lives. Banerjee and Ghosh (2012) also emphasize that training significantly influences various dimensions of empowerment, and the trained group members are more likely to be both empowered as well as employed.

One middle woman/agent from Paharkalan village when interviewed revealed that her husband used to beat her. She had interest in embroidery and this embroidery craft has been used by her in income generation when she joined the society. This craft has given her a lot. She has been able to provide education to her children. Now they are grown up and tell her not to work. She quoted her reply '*ye to meri pehchaan hai*' (it's my identity). Craft person's identity is often linked to the occupation that he/she follows (Gale and Kaur 2002). She gets work not only from this society but also gets order from the Patiala market individually. Initially she used to only embroider as an artisan, but now she also works as a middle agent. She has been able to face this world because of her interest in the craft and conversion of this craft into income generation activity. This identity has been useful in reshaping life of the craft person/artisan (Islam 2011).

Similar is the case of Shailinder Kaur (name changed), who was an artisan embroidering *dupattas* (long multipurpose scarf usually in light weight fabric and worn with *salwar kammez* in Punjab) few years back. She was not allowed by her mother-in-law to move out of her home freely. She had zero confidence. She enhanced her skills of embroidery when she joined a course of stitching and embroidery sponsored by KVIC in her village. She became instructor teaching embroidery to the girls in various villages. She then made a society with the help of NABARD. So far she has conducted workshops, started self-help groups in many villages and has helped around 1,500 women with this art. Her dream is to keep this art alive, teach as many women about this rich art and take it to an international level. This supports Al-Kharouf's (2010) argument that through embroidery some women are looking forward to set up their own ventures – be it a project or a fashion house or a Heritage Museum or production and publication of books. Shailinder Kaur added that all the self-help groups made by her are running successfully because she keeps in touch with all the members of the groups, continuously meets them, helps them in selling at stalls and in turn also gets a good reputation and earns more projects. She reported that her husband is a big support for her. She further added that her current status is also good and she is at such a platform for the reason that she wanted to grow in her life and has really worked hard to achieve it. I remember five years back when I met her for the first time, she had a low level of confidence, she could not talk properly and was very conscious while she was having conversation with me. Now she says that if anyone comes to their village and enquires about *phulkari* or embroidery, he/she is directed towards her house. Her name is now recognized by her profession which is her passion too. Nayak (1999) stresses that no external force will ever take women to a platform of stability, strength and solidarity till they develop the virtues within themselves and come out of the cage of their age-old weaknesses. Tikoo (1985) says government cannot be expected to bring about the coveted reforms or the upliftment of women, single-handedly unless they help themselves to translate those reforms into action.

Hall (1990) says that identity empowerment increases women's knowledge about their options in everyday life. Over time, they become more able to cope with conflict in their relationships, although initially they may be perceived by other people as being less productive or less cooperative than they were previously.

Embroidery for Spending Free Time

Almost 100 per cent artisans replied that women do embroidery not just because of interest but they want to spend their free time. They can't sit idle at their homes or watch TV for a long duration. Cooking does not involve much time, kids go off to school in the morning, and husbands also move out after the breakfast, they are free after that, they sit together and embroider.

The artisan reported that the ladies who join self-help groups are usually from a low socio-economic background. Husbands of many women are into the habit of drinking, many are earning less, many have large families which drive these women to work as they also think *'vele bai kar ki karna'* (It's better to work rather than sitting idle). Embroidery is also an activity for spending time constructively and creatively. It is a stress buster for many artisans. When women embroider together sitting with neighbours or friends, it is a platform to discuss their routine, joys, sorrows, problems etc. They tend to find out solution for their problems.

Another woman interviewed was from Rajpura, in Patiala district and is in the profession of *phulkari* for nearly 15 years. She gets embroidery done on *dupattas* and *suits* from the artisans in various villages and sells these further. When she became *sarpanch* of her village, she encouraged women to embroider as they had lot of free time and they used to sit idle and fight over their children. She says rural women who are involved with this profession are now able to deposit school fee of their children and they are able to save some amount for themselves. In fact when women embroider and earn, their mothers-in-law also feel happy as their daughters-in-law are not sitting idle and can buy their own *suits* or fulfill their requirements themselves according to their choice *'apna karcha khudd nikal sakti hain'* (they can manage their own expenses). For her too, this embroidery as a profession gives a lot of satisfaction *'jis kam nu karke mann nu santushti miley, oho kam bahut acha hai'* (work which gives you satisfaction is a perfect work). Sahay (1998) mentions that at psychological level, people who become more empowered, feel better about themselves, there is an increased sense of personal dignity, self-respect and self-esteem. This was observed with many more women involved with embroidery and *phulkari* making. Earning profit is not her (woman interviewed) aim for pursuing this profession. Through this activity she is able to spend some good time in the company of her friends and neighbours. She feels satisfied that with this work artisans become self-sufficient.

Embroidery as a Constructive–Collective Effort in the Form of Self-Help Groups

An exhibition organized by CII in Chandigarh in the year 2012 was visited. Many self-help groups participated in this fair where stalls were allocated for the display and sale of the products.

Sharma (2012) defines self-help group as a small homogenous and affinity group of rural poor generally not exceeding twenty members, voluntarily coming together with the motive of saving small amounts regularly, contributing to a common fund for meeting their emergency needs, collective decision making, solving conflicts through collective leadership and mutual discussion.

Jyoti Self-Help Group and Narivikas Self-Help Group got one collective stall in this fair where they displayed hand embroidered *dupattas*, *suits*, bed sheets etc. One artisan (also a middle woman) from village Faridpur Jattan was member of Narivikas Self-Help Group of 15 members. She is making *phulkari* since last seventeen years. Their group got loan, and out of fifteen members ten members collectively embroidered and prepared articles for this fair. Another woman from village Kalomajra was a member of Jyoti Self-Help Group. Their experience of working together as a group and then participating in the fair was wonderful as they were able to interact with a lot of people in the fair and also got appreciation from the public visiting the stall. They were feeling shy in the beginning of the fair but after few days they were able to talk and deal with the customers/public easily and confidently. They mentioned that they have gained a lot other than just improving upon their skills of embroidery. They said '*hum khul kar jine lag gaye hain*' (we have started living freely). Such collective efforts of women not only empowers them but is also a source of gaining capacity in other fields like learning new skills, gaining command over language, decision-making (Dol and Odame 2013) collective efficacy, self-esteem and independence (Moyle, Dollard and Biswas 2006).

The Director of 'The Patiala Handloom Handicraft Workshop Cooperative Industrial Society Ltd.' also remarked that self-help groups have been created in villages where around 10–11 women collect and start contributing as a saving. According to her, 'Our society has created self-help groups in villages. We teach these women to help themselves. They should not be asking anyone for money'. Every women of this group contributes some amount per month. They also inter-loan within the group, when required. These women are also helped to take loan from the banks to start some work of their own. Utilizing the loan, they can invest in the raw material to prepare the product and can collectively prepare various products and sell them in various fairs/exhibitions. Hence slowly and slowly they earn and gain confidence and are able to spend on themselves and their children and on many others in their households. 'We make/transform these ladies to be self-dependent'. Above all, this helps them develop a feeling of in-group solidarity. Many scholars have advocated that by joining hands with each other through formation of self-help groups, women get empowered to participation, economic empowerment and capacity building (Das 2012) and hence reducing their dependence on money lenders (Galab and Rao 2003).

Narratives in this research article have confirmed role of embroidery as an agency for empowerment of women. Traditional crafts that were part of woman's life since times unknown have now become part of process that gives housewives a sense of distinctive identity, a resource for monetary mobilization and provides additional income to meet her personal and family's requirements. It brings change in her domestic position – she starts getting respect from other power centres in the house (in most cases mother-in-law) and if she is a single mother, her children draw inspiration from her ability to utilize her skill for productivity. Group activities are invariably a source of entertainment, they provide legitimacy for a natural human desire to unwind and gossip acquires attributes of productive labour. These contexts help us to relocate *phulkari* not only as a traditional craft and heritage from Punjab but have also provided a context and agency for exploring enabling abilities of this subtle craft.

REFERENCES

Al-Dajani, Haya and Susan Marlow (2010) 'Impact of Women's Home-Based Enterprise on Family Dynamics: Evidence from Jordan', *International Small Business Journal*, 28 (5).

Al-Kharouf, Amal (2010) 'The Role of the Art of Embroidery in the Economic Empowerment of Women', *Jordan Journal of the Arts*, 3 (1).

Banerjee, Tanmoyee and Chandralekha Ghosh (2012) 'What Factors Play a Role in Empowering Women? A Study of SHG Members from India', *Gender Technology and Development*, 16 (3).

Boerema, Christina, Mary Russell and Alejandra Aguilar (2010) 'Sewing in the Lives of Immigrant Women', *Journal of Occupational Science*, 17 (2).

Brijbhushan, J. (1990) *Indian Embroidery*. New Delhi: Director, Publications Division, Ministry of Information and Broadcasting, Government of India.

Christiansen, Charles H. (1999) 'Defining Lives: Occupation as Identity: An Essay on Competence, Coherence and the Creation of Meaning', *American Journal of Occupational Therapy*, 53 (6).

Das, Sanjay Kanti (2012) 'Microfinance and Women Empowerment: Does Self-Help Group Empowers Women?', *International Journal of Management and Business Studies*, 2 (2).

Datta, Rekha (2003) 'From Development to Empowerment: The Self-Employed Women's Association in India', *International Journal of Politics, Culture and Society*, 16 (3).

Devasia, L. and V.V. Devasia (1994) *Empowering Women for Sustainable Development*. New Delhi: Ashish Publishing House.

Dhamija, Jasleen (2004) Embroidery: An Expression of Women's Creativity. In Jasleen Dhamija (Ed.) *Asian Embroidery*. Delhi: Abhinav Publications.

Dol, Justine and Helen Hambly Odame (2013) 'Stitching Toward Empowerment: A Case Study of Tabiro Ladies' Club', *Journal of Co-operative Organization and Management*, 1 (2).

Edwards, Clive (2006) 'Home is Where the Art is: Women, Handicrafts and Home Improvements 1750–1900', *Journal of Design History*, 19 (1).

Emeneau, Murray Barnson (1937) 'Toda Garments and Embroidery', *Journal of the American Oriental Society*, 57 (3).

Galab, S. and N. Chandrasekhara Rao (2003) 'Women's Self-Help Groups, Poverty Alleviation and Empowerment', *Economic and Political Weekly*, 38 (12–13).

Gale, C. and J. Kaur (2002) *The Textile Book*. New York: Berg.

Gupta, C.S. (2010) Picturesque Frame of Non-Cognitive Expression: Phulkari. In K. Vatsyayan (Ed.), *Embroidery in Asia Sui Dhaga: Crossing Boundaries through Needle and Thread*. New Delhi: Wisdom Tree.

Hall, Constance Margaret (1990) 'Identity Empowerment through Clinical Sociology', *Clinical Sociology Review*, 8.

Islam, Rafiqul (2011) 'Rural Women's Empowerment through Self-Income Generating Activities: A Study on NGO Development Programs in Bangladesh', *Journal of Global Citizenship and Equity Education*, 1 (1).

Laliberte-Rudman, Debbie (2002) 'Linking Occupation and Identity: Lessons Learned through Qualitative Exploration', *Journal of Occupational Science*, 9 (1).

Menon, L. (1998) *Women Empowerment and Challenge of Change*. New Delhi: Kanishka Publishers & Distributors.

Mitra, J. (1997) *Women and Society: Equality and Empowerment*. New Delhi: Kanishka Publishers, Distributors.

Moyle, Tracy L., Maureen Dollard and Saswata Narayan Biswas (2006) 'Personal and Economic Empowerment in Rural Indian Women: A Self-Help Group Approach', *International Journal of Rural Management*, 2 (2).

Nayak, U. (1999) *Women's Development and Social Conflicts: Historical Perspectives on Indian Women: Study in Orissa*. New Delhi: Kanishka Publishers & Distributors.

Noopur, I.K. (1989) *Women's Studies in School Education: A New Perspective*. New Delhi: Sterling Publishers (P) Ltd.

Parker, R. (1984) *The Subversive Stitch: Embroidery and the Making of the Feminine*. London: The Women's Press.

Pillai, J.K. (1995) *Women and Empowerment*. New Delhi: Gyan Publishing House.

Raheim, Salome and Jacquelyn Bolden (1995) 'Economic Empowerment of Low-Income Women through Self-Employment Programs', *Affilia*, 10 (2).

Randhawa, Varinder and Sukhdeep Kaur Mann (2005) 'Empowerment of Women through Self-Help Groups in Punjab', *Journal of Dairying, Foods and Home Sciences*, 24 (3–4).

Reynolds, Frances (2003) 'Reclaiming a Positive Identity in Chronic Illness through Artistic Occupation', *Occupational Therapy Journal of Research*, 23 (3).

Riley, Jillian (2008) 'Weaving an Enhanced Sense of Self and a Collective Sense of Self through Creative Textile-Making', *Journal of Occupational Science*, 15 (2).

Sahay, S. (1998) *Women and Empowerment: Approaches and Strategies*. New Delhi: Discovery Publishing House Pvt. Ltd.

Sharma, A. (2012) *Women Empowerment through Microfinance and SHGs*. New Delhi: Sonali Publications.

Singh, initials??? (2010) A Wrap of Blessings. In K. Vatsyayan (Ed.) *Embroidery in Asia Sui Dhaga: Crossing Boundaries through Needle and Thread*. New Delhi: Wisdom Tree.

The World Bank (2013) http://web.worldbank.org/wbsite/external/topics/extpoverty/extempowerment/0,,contentmdk:20245753~pagepk:210058~pipk:210062~thesitepk:486411,00.html (Retrieved on 20 January 2014)

Tikoo, P.N. (1985) *Indian Women: A Brief Socio-Cultural Survey*. Delhi: B.R. Publishing Corporation.

Unruh, Anita M. (2004) 'Reflections on: So...What Do You Do? Occupation and the Construction of Identity', *Canadian Journal of Occupational Therapy*, 71 (5).

Warin, Megan and Simone Dennis (2005) 'Threads of Memory: Reproducing the Cypress Tree through Sensual Consumption', *Journal of Intercultural Studies*, 26 (1–2).

6

Implications of Rural Tourism to Chinese Rural Women's Subjective Well-Being

XIANG YIXIAO AND DONG ISBISTER

It is well noted that tourism is an industry that highly involves rural female employment (Fan, Zhen and Ding 2007; McGehee, Kim and Jennings 2006). A recently emerging body of western literature was found in the cross-area of rural tourism and gender analysis focused on the motivation of rural females involving rural tourism, different operation models of rural female entrepreneurship, rural tourism bringing the rural female's invisible side-work to light and the positive effect on their mentality etc. (Markantoni and van Hoven 2012; Koutsou et al. 2009; McGehee, Kim and Jennings 2006). Unlike these western literature discussing relations of rural tourism and rural females in a more diversified paradigm, Chinese research on rural tourism and rural women are mainly focused on the financial impact of the former on the latter, considering the context of pro-poor tourism (PPT) strategy in rural China launched by the Chinese government (Liu 2007; Fan, Zhen and Ding 2007; Lin and Ding 2009; Zheng, Zhou and Zhu 2012), an in-depth study of the well-being of the rural females in relation to rural tourism development in China can hardly be found in the existing literature. The authors argue that what tourism development in the rural areas brings to the local females is far more than financial benefits, and that it is meaningful to inquire about the multifaceted impacts of tourism on the local rural female life so as to ensure the sustainability of tourism itself and the well-being of the females in rural China. To address the gap, this exploratory study examines what are the implications of rural tourism development in the two villages near the city of Jinan, China, to the subjective well-being of the rural female villagers who take it as an alternative livelihood means.

Related Concepts

It is necessary, in the first place, to clarify the concepts of subjective well-being and rural tourism – *Nongjiale* that theoretically and instrumentally guidelines this research.

Well-being and Subjective Well-being

Well-being is generally viewed as a description of the state of people's life situation (McGillivray 2007). Well-being was traditionally identified with a single objective dimension, i.e. material well-being, measured by income or GDP. However, with the deepening of study in this realm, well-being measurements evolved to include broader dimensions such as socio-environmental aspects and human rights, and then expanded to be even more multidimensional which encompassed all aspects of human life (Conceicao and Bandura 2014; Sumner 2006; McGillivray 2007). In this case, indicators in areas such as education, health and nutrition, environment, empowerment and participation have been advocated to complement GDP for well-being measurement. However, with the growing criticism on indicators for oversimplifying complex reality and lacking transparency in methodologies, subjective measures emerged as a new approach to measuring multidimensional well-being (Easterlin 2004).

According to Diener et al. (1964), subjective well-being (SWB) refers to how people experience the quality of their lives and includes both emotional reactions and cognitive judgments. Happiness is defined as a combination of satisfaction in life and the relative frequency of positive and negative affect, and therefore SWB entails moods, emotions and evaluations of one's satisfaction with general and specific areas of one's life (Diener et al. 1999). Bruni and Porta (2007) further identify SWB into four components: 1) pleasant emotions, 2) unpleasant emotions, 3) global life judgment (life evaluation), and 4) domain satisfaction (marriage, health, leisure etc.). Subjective well-being is usually observed through questions about individual's 'happiness' or 'life satisfaction' (van Praag et al. 2003). Life satisfaction reflects individuals' perceived distance from their aspirations while happiness results from a balance between positive and negative affect. In another word, SWB is a synonym of 'being happy' whereas concepts such as 'satisfaction' and 'happiness' are considered 'feeling happy' (Bruni and Porta 2007).

Researchers identify determinants to assist measuring subjective well-being. The determinants are grouped into either objective and subjective ones, economic and non-economic ones, or internal and external ones (Conceicao and Bandura 2014; Schimmack 2006), the effort of which is to measure SWB in most comprehensive and valid way as it can be. Diener and Suh (1997) note that despite the conceptual and methodological differences between social indicators and SWB, scientific approaches to well-being need to take a comprehensive view of the phenomenon by incorporating the strengths of each perspective. For the purpose of this research, both social/objective indicators and subjective ones will be adopted to measure the SWB of the rural women in China under the impact of rural tourism development.

Rural Tourism and Nongjiale

Rural tourism is tourism that takes place in the countryside (Lane 1994). According to both Lane (1994) and Organization for Economic Co-operation and Development (OECD 1994), rural tourism should be built upon the rural world's special features of small-scale enterprises, open spaces, natural heritage, traditional societies and traditional practices. It allows visitors' personalized contact and participation in the activities, traditions and lifestyles of the local people. It should often be very largely controlled locally and developed for the long-term good of the locals with a high percentage of tourism revenue benefiting the rural local community.

Nongjiale, as a distinctive Chinese version of rural tourism (Su 2011) takes place in the rural and suburban area around the skirt of the Chinese cities where urban visitor can drive to and fro within a day or two so to purchase and experience the tourism products developed there (Sia et al. 2013; Su 2011; Zhao, Ritchie and Echtner 2011). This promotion of rural ways of life and cultures which are mainly featured with home-made meals well responds to the postmodern tourists' quest for authenticity (Urry 2002), and meanwhile encourages the local villagers to participate in and benefit from serving or hosting visitors. The rural tourism destinations across mainland China accommodated and entertained more than 300 million of tourists per year, and generated 40 billion RMB in revenue (Shao 2007). According to Shao and official statistics of the Chinese National Tourism Administration (CNTA) (2007), every year during the two 'Golden Weeks' (1–7 May and 1–7 October), about 70 per cent of urban residents (about 60 millions) nationwide would take a rural tour, creating a huge market of rural tourism, and accordingly producing a high percentage of employment for the rural female population (Fan, Zhen and Ding 2007; Liu 2007).

Research Context

Nongjiale and Rural Females in China

Rural tourism in the form of *Nongjiale* boomed and developed drastically in China thanks to following three major factors. One, urbanization and stressful urban life catalyses the urban dwellers' desire for embracing the nature and relaxing by the experience of idyllic rural lifestyle which generates high demand, and the surrounding rural *Nongjiale* makes ideal destinations featured with low cost of both time and money. Two, rapid urban sprawl, meanwhile, invades and occupies vast rural land in the recent decade of China and causes a population of 51–55 million to lose their land and consequently lose their traditional livelihoods, with a forecast that the number of landless population will increase to 100 million by 2020 (Li 2009, Zhang 2010). Three, how to help these landless farmers resettle becomes a serious challenge to governments of varied levels and rural tourism as pro-poor tourism is adopted as an important strategy that will address this problem and alleviate poverty in rural China.

Fan, Zhen and Ding (2007) noted that among the *Nongjiale* employed populace, approximately 55 per cent are rural females, and in the case of Zhoucheng village of Dali, Yunan province resided mainly by ethnic groups, statistical data shows the number of mature labour in the village as around 3,000 but the female villagers aged from 10 to 70 who are actually involved in tourism service to varied degrees have amounted to 4,500. The situation is more or less similar in other rural areas of China where tourism, or *Nongjiale*, is developed. The rural-urban migration of the rural male labour force may account for this reality. However, on the other hand, it well reflects the great potential of female women as sustained human resource to rural tourism development in China, and as well the importance of the role and contribution of rural women in rural tourism operations. The well-being of the rural females hence makes a valuable subject for study.

Research Site

This research chooses two villages, Ouchi village and Shangjianggan village in the southern mountainous area, just 20 kms, away from Jinan, China, where *Nongjiale* was started 10 years ago and saw a rapid and steady growth in the recent years. Both the villages are under the jurisdiction of Xiying county of Jinan city, the capital city of Shandong Province, China. The villages were selected for two reasons – convenience of accessibility; and the fact that both the villages are relatively rich in rural tourism resource and mature in *Nongjiale* development. Ouchi has a 13.7 kms, hiking/cycling route going through the village and a vast chestnut plantation of about 10,000 Mu (about 6.67 square kilometres) adjacent to the village, while Shangjianggan is located at the foot of Yunti Mountain which is 976 km above the sea level and ranks as the second highest mountain in Shandong province just next to Mount Taishan which is a world heritage site. To encourage *Nongjiale*, the hiking route, the chestnut plantation, and the mountain are all open, free to attract close-by urban visitors coming over for outdoor activities and to enjoy the home-made meal and buy local organic products prepared by the local villagers. Official data from Xiying town government reveals that in 2012, the tourist reception by the *Nongjiale* restaurants in the town was 7,00,000 with a total revenue of ¥70 million RMB (about $11.5 million USD), and the tourist reception number of the first half of 2013 reached 2,13,000 with a revenue of ¥51 million RMB (about $8.31 million USD), showing an increase of 12.2 per cent and 15.5 per cent respectively. Statistics also reveals that over 80 per cent of the *Nongjiale* related labour force is female (Xiying Tourism Office 2013).

Shangjianggan village has 51 families totaling 243 people but around two thirds, mainly males, are out working in the cities. Ouchi has 45 families totaling 207 people and with similar situation as Shangjianggan that the majority of the family member staying in the village are women, aged men and the children. The two villages make typical cases for examining Chinese rural females' well-being and its relation to rural tourism development in their place.

Research Methods and Data Collection

To obtain valid and in-depth data, both qualitative and quantitative methods are adopted in this research. A questionnaire survey was designed and conducted in the two villages; semi-structure interviews and in-depth interviews were conducted. Participatory observations were also conducted in the field.

Data collection in the field went on in two phases: The first round of fieldwork was done on 1–3 November 2013, during which a questionnaire survey was done in the two villages with the villagers with the help of the town and village committee leaders; and semi-structure interviews were conducted with 16 families, 10 in Shangjianggan and 6 in Ouchi. Each semi-structured interview lasted about 7–10 minutes. Among the 16 interviews, 5 were with female villagers who were not involved in *Nongjiale* catering service. The second round data collection took place on 16–18 February 2014, mainly with follow-up, in-depth interviews with the families interviewed in the first round. Around 9 interviews in total, 6 in Shangjianggan and 3 in Ouchi were conducted and this round was based on the availability of the interviewees. Each in-depth interview lasted about 30–40 minutes and the interviewees are all *Nongjiale*-involved females.

Taking reference of OECD guidelines on measuring subjective well-being, considering the special objective of this research as examining the implication of rural tourism on the rural female's subjective well-being, the questionnaire survey is structured into three parts: (1) two questions are asked for self-reported overall happiness and life satisfaction (all things considered), using Cantril's Ladder of Life Scale with 0–10 steps of ladders; (2) 14 specific questions were asked about happiness based on a 5 point Likert scale that are designed based on 4 determinants including democratic, economic, socio-cultural, and environmental ones within the context and function of Nongjiale development; and (3) demographic characters of the interviewees.

About 60 copies of questionnaires were distributed to the villagers of the two villages while village meetings were convened. Around 45 copies were collected and 39 were valid. Although the samples are not sufficient for a decent analysis but we have tried to extract valuable information and connections from them.

Semi-structured and in-depth questions are mainly focused on 'how' and 'why' about the information obtained from the questionnaire survey, examining the relation of their perceived well-being and rural tourism.

Data Presentation and Analysis

The data obtained from both the questionnaire survey and the interviews are sorted, categorized and presented as follows.

The questionnaire survey is composed of three sections: Section A contains two questions asking about overall perceptions of happiness and life satisfaction; Section B contains 14 questions asking about perceptions of happiness in relation to tourism involvement; Section C collects demographic data of the interviewees.

The demographic data obtained from Section C of the questionnaire surveys reveal that among 39 survey interviewees there were only 5 male members of the two villages and the rest were all female aging from 16 to 64. Ignoring the 5 males, demographic details of the female villagers are presented in Table 1.

Table 1
Demographic Information of the Surveyed/Interviewed Female Villagers

Age	*16–29*	*30–45*	*46–59*	*60 and above*
Sample No.	7 (20.6%)	13 (38.2%)	10 (29.4%)	4 (11.8%)
Education	Primary	Junior	High	College
Sample No.	10 (29.4%)	18 (53.0%)	6 (17.6%)	0 (0%)
Annual income	15,000 and under	15,000–60,000	60,000–1,00,000	1,00,000 and above
Sample No.	5 (14.7%)	16 (47.1%)	10 (29.4%)	3 (8.8%)
Employment	Tourism	Others	None	
Sample No.	29 (85.3%)	3 (8.8%)	2	

Overall Happiness and Life Satisfaction of the Rural Females

For Section A of the questionnaire survey, Cantril's Ladder of Life Scale and World Values Survey were adopted with the following questions being asked:

1. Please imagine a ladder with steps numbered from zero at the bottom to ten at the top. Suppose we say that the top of the ladder represents the best possible life for you and the bottom of the ladder represents the worst possible life for you.
   If the top step is 10 and the bottom step is 0, on which step of the ladder do you feel you personally stand at the present time? (0–10)
2. The following question asks how happy you feel, on a scale from 0 to 10. Zero means you feel 'not at all happy' and 10 means 'completely happy'.
   Taking all things together, how happy would you say you are? (0–10)

The result of the survey data is sorted as seen in Table 2, which shows that the majority of the survey interviewees, 76.8 per cent, perceive themselves at scale 6–7, a fairly good state of happiness and life satisfaction on the whole.

Table 2
Overall Happiness and Life Satisfaction of Female Survey Interviewees

Indicators	*Scale 0–10*									
Perceived Happiness	0	0	0	1	3	11	15	4	0	0
Frequency %	0	0	0	2.9	8.8	32.4	44.1	11.8	0	0
Life Satisfaction	0	0	0	2	6	14	10	2	0	0
Frequency %	0	0	0	5.9	17.6	41.2	29.4	5.9	0	0

Rural Females' Perception of Happiness in Relation to Tourism Involvement

For Section B of the questionnaire survey, determinants are grouped into four categories such as democratic, economic, socio-cultural, and environmental aspects within the context and function of *Nongjiale* development. Under each category sub-level indicators are extracted based on which questions or positive statements (Q/S) are designed based on 5-point Likert scales. Section B ends with two overall questions/statements about their perception of happiness in relation to tourism involvement. The interviewees' responses are coded with cardinal numbers ranging from 5 for 'totally agree', 4 for 'agree', 3 for 'hard to say', 2 for 'disagree', to 1 for 'totally disagree'.

Questions/statements (Q/S) under democracy category are about empowerment relevant to family and community issues, freedom of choice, and equal opportunities of tourism participation; Q/S under socio-cultural category are about identity, attachment to the community, and family and social relation; Q/S under economic category are about tourism income and economic independence, tourism income and family life, and employment and confidence; Q/S under environment category are about village resource's environment, tourism pollution, and convenience of life. The results are presented in Table 3.

The interviewees' responses to the 12 questions are presented in Table 3. Judging from the data generated, one may note that generally speaking the majority of the interviewed rural female villagers perceive a very positive relation of their happiness and life satisfaction with *Nongjiale* (79.4% and 64.7%). About 73.5 per cent of them agree that *Nongjiale* makes them more empowered. About 61.8 per cent of them feel that they have more freedom of choice in life. More than 70 per cent of them agree that they are aware of a stronger gender and social identity as well as feel a sense of attachment to their home village and community through involvement in *Nongjiale*. Also, more than 70 per cent of them agree that tourism income enables their independence and enhances their family life, and more than half of them (52.9%) agree that getting employed in *Nongjiale* makes them feel more self-confident. Only 11.8 per cent of them think resource and environment are impacted by tourism and less than half of them (41.2%) are bothered by pollution caused by tourism. On the contrary, an overwhelming majority (91.2%) agree that tourism brings more convenience to their life with the infrastructure improvement. It should also be noted that only 41.2 per cent of them agree that tourism provides equal opportunities of participation.

Table 3

Interviewees' Responses about Tourism and the Female Survey Interviewees SWB and Tourism

Questions/ Statements	*Frequency and Percentage*				
	Totally Disagree	*Disagree*	*Hard to Say*	*Agree*	*Totally Agree*
More empowerment	0 (0%)	2 (5.9%)	7 (20.6%)	17 (50%)	8 (23.5%)
More freedom of life choice	1 (2.9%)	4 (11.8%)	8 (23.5%)	16 (47.1%)	5 (14.7%)
More equal participation	3 (8.8%)	9 (26.5)	3 (8.8%)	15 (29.4%)	4 (11.8%)
Stronger identity	0 (0%)	1 (2.9%)	7 (20.6%)	19 (55.9%)	7 (20.6%)
Community attachment	1 (2.9%)	4 (11.8%)	5 (14.7%)	17 (50%)	7 (20.6%)
Family and social relation	2 (5.9%)	5 (14.7%)	5 (14.7%)	17 (50%)	5 (14.7%)
Income and independence	1 (2.9%)	2 (5.9%)	5 (14.7%)	17 (50%)	9 (26.5%)
Income and family life	1 (2.9%)	3 (8.8%)	6 (17.6%)	18 (52.9%)	6 (17.6%)
Employment and confidence	3 (8.8%)	6 (17.6%)	7 (20.6%)	13 (38.2%)	5 (14.7%)

Cont'd...

...Cont'd

Resource and environment	2 (5.9%)	2 (5.9%)	5 (14.7%)	20 (58.8%)	5 (14.7%)
Severe tourism pollution	7 (20.6%)	10 (29.4%)	7 (20.6%)	12 (35.3%)	2 (5.9%)
More convenience of life	0 (0%)	1 (2.9%)	2 (5.9%)	22 (64.7)	9 (26.5%)
Involvement in tourism makes me feel happy	0 (0%)	3 (8.8%)	4 (11.8%)	23 (67.6%)	4 (11.8%)
Satisfaction with changes tourism brings to life	0 (0%)	5 (14.7 %)	7 (20.6 %)	21 (61.8%)	1 (2.9%)

Around 16 semi-structured interviews and 9 follow-up, in-depth interviews were taken (partly digital recorded with permission) and transcribed, which highlights some of the questions and issues that were not addressed in the questionnaire surveys. The data was grouped into 7 themes and the information of the interviews is presented in Table 4.

Table 4

Information of the Interviewees

Villages	*Shangjianggan (SJG)*		*Ouchi (OCH)*	
Interviewees	10		6	
Age	16–29	30–45	46–59	60 and above
Interviewees	3	8	4	1
Education	primary	junior	high	college
Interviewees	2	10	4	0
Employment with Nongjiale	restaurant owner	waitress	others	none
Interviewees	7	4	3	2
Annual income	15,000 and under	15,000–60,000	60,000–1,00,000	1,00,000 and above
Interviewees	4	7	4	1
Marriage status	married with spouse at home	married with spouse not at home	single	divorced or widowed

Cont'd...

...Cont'd

Interviewees	3	7	3	3
Kids per family	one kid	two kids	three kids	four kids
Interviewees	3	8	5	0
Types and length of interviews	semi-structured interviews, 7–10 minutes		in-depth interviews, 30–40 minutes	
Interviewees	16 (10 in SJG and 6 in OCH)		9 (6 in SJG and 3 in OCH)	

By analysing the interview data, 7 themes that emerged are as follows:

1. Nongjiale, Economic Independence and SWB

Both the semi-structured interviews and in-depth interviews unanimously indicate that being involved in serving *Nongjiale* brings them significant income increase which gives them more economic independence. According to one of the interviewees, '*With the money I earned in tourism serving I can buy small items my children need for schooling and my family needs in daily life, without having to ask my husband for money*, 'Many of them feel good as they have more freedom of choices in dealing with family affairs with money in hands and that makes life easier and happier. '*I spent ¥150 having my hair made. He (husband) did not complain. He used to be picky with how I should or should not spend money*' said an interviewee who now owns a small *Nongjiale* restaurant. She is happy that they don't have to quarrel over those financial trifles as before.

2. Nongjiale, Empowerment and SWB

If increased income encourages economic empowerment, then empowerment that *Nongjiale* brings to the rural females is more than that. It is noted that interviewees involved in *Nongjiale* are more extrovert and self-confident than those who are not involved. These women are friendly and talkative which makes the interviews go smoothly, at many times like casual chatting. We believe this positive personality is somewhat cultivated thanks to serving and interacting with tourists. The majority of the interviewees express that they now have a better say in family issues as they play both the traditional female role of taking care of the family and male role of making money. Asked about participation in community issues, 6 of the interviewees said that they had several occasions to attend the village meetings discussing *Nongjiale* related issue and believed it is important to get updated information which is helpful for their businesses. It is noted that the 2 interviewees not involved in *Nongjiale* are not so enthusiastic talking about it, although they admitted they can sell local agro-products to tourists and make some money at home. One interviewee points out that the village committee supports the villagers to participate in *Nongjiale* selectively. She does not enjoy equal opportunities to get involved.

3. Nongjiale, Family Life and SWB

Family life, husband, children, and aged parents are still rated the most important part by the interviewees who are of age 30 years and above. One reason that most of them feel happy about *Nongjiale* is that they don't have to leave their kids and parents at home like their husband to go to the cities hunting for a job. '*I am happy I can take care of my family and meanwhile make money at home*' said one interviewee who runs a small *Nongjiale* restaurant. Two of them are particularly positive about *Nongjiale* because after their *Nongjiale* business started and developed, their husbands realized they can make as much (if not more) money being involved with *Nongjiale* at home, as they make working in the city. Now the husband is the chef and in charge of purchasing materials while the wife is the accountant and serves the tourists with the help of a locally hired waitress. They make good business while enjoying reunited family life.

4. Nongjiale, Identity and Place Attachment and SWB

Although not used to the term 'identity', almost all the female villagers interviewed admit *Nongjiale* helps them know themselves, their culture and traditions, and their home village better. One villager said, 'I did not know I am capable to do it *(Nongjiale)* before I started. I did not realize my village is so good before the tourists repeatedly told me. What we take for granted is fascinating in the tourists' eyes, the rooster, the goat, the orchard, and couplets on the door, and the stone mill outside the yard. I am glad I can relook at them and appreciate their value through the tourists' eyes. Many tourists come, bring big plastic container to collect the spring water to take home, and say it is very precious for making tea. We drink such spring water everyday! .... I love this village and feel good living in it'. A young female waitress also expressed similar feeling. She said the village was poor when her sister got married, and she married a man in a far, richer village. She does not have to follow her sisters' way. She is in love with a young man in the village who is now in the city as a migrant worker and they will get married when the young man earned enough money to build a house for them. 'We will stay in the village. I am proud that many girls from the nearby villages want to marry our boys and live in our village. When we save enough money, we will build a new style *Nongjiale* or set up some other business of our own'. These young people actually represent the hope and future of the villages as well as the future of rural tourism.

5. Nongjiale, Environment and SWB

Observation in the field revealed quite a few problems of resource and environmental stress caused by *Nongjiale* and tourist. For example, tourists usually drive over with families. Parking space becomes a big problem. It is mentioned in the interview that quarrels and fights take place for parking space during high seasons. The river going through the village at Shangjianggan and the pond at Ouchi are all polluted in varied degrees with a lot of floated green alga and other dirty things and with a bad smell when going close to the water. The river or pond water comes from the mountain springs and, as one villager said, they used to use the water for drinking and cooking. But now it is not drinkable at all and village families have to use plastic pipes as aqueduct to get water from the mountain down to their houses.

However, when asked about water pollution, crowd and noise in high seasons, interviewees did not have any strong responses. To our concern, these problems do not seem to impact much on their feeling of well-being and their positive attitude toward tourism. They have yet to realize the severe consequence of the environmental cost, and are very friendly and welcoming to tourists. '*The more tourists, the better*', said one of the interviewees. This can well be explained with Doxey's irritation index – the relation between the villagers and *Nongjiale* are still in the 'euphoria' stage. Many of them mention that they enjoy the convenience brought by the infrastructure development for *Nongjiale* rural tourism such as the road, bus route, electricity, etc.

6. Nongjiale, Personal Growth and SWB

A considerable number of interviewees mentioned that involvement in *Nongjiale* service is a learning and growing process. A female *Nongjiale* owner in her mid-forties said she enjoyed interacting with tourists, 'I like to explore and develop recipes and feel very happy and proud when tourists praise my dishes. A sense of achievement, you know. I like to talk to tourists and listen to them talking while serving them. They are just like a window open to me and leading me to the outside world. I feel my life is enriched'. Another interviewee who is a 18-year-old waitress said, 'My mom told me I've really grown up with the 6 months of serving tourists at my auntie's restaurant. I also think so. I feel I am more thoughtful and capable to work and deal with people. I am more comfortable with who I am and more confident to go and survive in the cities. I am happy with this'.

7. Other Findings about Nongjiale and Rural Female SWB

A big concern of 9 interviewees is that *Nongjiale*, though beneficial, has taken so much of their time and energy that they can barely take good care of their children's education and growth. They reported problems with their kids such as not regularly attending school, failure in exams, difficulty in mutual communication, and teenager rebellions. Some of them feel that although they did not mean to, but actually have ignored their children's growth. Despite this, they feel that it is still better than going out to work in the cities while leaving their kids at home with the aged grandparents.

Data also reveal that among the 4 relatively successful female entrepreneurs in *Nongjiale* (with annual income above ¥70,000 RMB), 3 have High School education and one has Junior High School education. It is noted that interviewees with lower level of education tend to have less confidence and are not so positive at expressing their ideas.

When asked about their expectations, almost all the interviewees expressed need of government support in detailed terms of financial funding, policy support, and skills training, etc.

Discussion

Synthesizing the quantitative and qualitative data analysed above, we maintain that, the implication of *Nongjiale* on the rural females is far more than income increase. It impacts the well-being of the rural females in varied but more positive than negative ways. The research finding is discussed in the following aspects.

Rural Women's SWB is Closely Correlated with Rural Tourism Development in their Local Habitats

In the Chinese context of urbanization, land loss, loss of traditional livelihoods, rural-urban migration, and other challenges, rural tourism, with *Nongjiale* as its most popular form, is introduced by the government as an alternative livelihood as well an alleviation strategy to address rural problems in China. Women become the major labour force left in much of the rural area and hence play a key role in *Nongjiale* development. In the cases of this research, the relatively high scale of their overall happiness and life satisfaction and their positive attitude toward *Nongjiale* show that the rural females demonstrate their high potential of adapting to the changes in their life and turn challenges into opportunities. *Nongjiale* not only brings income and employment to the rural females, but also has other profound implications in their life.

1. It moves them from an invisible and subordinated back corner to the front stage as a key role. This earns them more respect and empowerment. They enjoy higher status and have a better say among their family members, and in some cases among their community members as well. The economic independence makes them feel more confident and comfortable to express their opinions and aspirations.
2. Through serving and interacting with the visitors, they acquire a new angle to look at themselves and have a stronger awareness of their own identity and a better recognition of the value of their local culture and traditions, and therefore a stronger attachment to their villages.
3. Family has been rated the most important part by women's life, especially the rural females in China due to the long historic role they play and the traditional sense of value that

they are inculcated with, and thus the quality of family life weighs high in their self-evaluation on happiness and satisfaction. *Nongjiale* development not only brings economic well-being to the rural females' family, but also has a great potential of attracting their husbands back from the cities to join them in the tourism service business. The return of the male family member alleviates the females' intensity of work, gives them more time to take care of the kids and the aged members. More importantly, family reunion plays a significant role in enhancing the quality of family life of the rural females and hence their subjective well-being.

4. *Nongjiale* and tourists open a window for the rural females to know about the outside world, enlarge their scope of knowledge and vision, and release their potentials. Female leadership building is distinctly exhibited through *Nongjiale* businesses. The involved women are more knowledgeable in management skills and more competent dealing with issues arising in their operations through years of practical training. Meanwhile, increased knowledge, enlarged vision, enriched experience acquired by interacting with tourist helps them in dealing with their family relations and issues also.

All these constitute comprehensive measures for the subjective well-being of the rural females and indicated that *Nongjiale* development has a positive influence on the well-being of the rural women. Nevertheless, a couple of issues are identified in this research that, if not properly addressed, may negatively affect their long-term well-being, even if presently not fully recognized.

Issues that Need Consideration in Measuring the SWB of Chinese Rural Females in Relation to Nongjiale

1. The impact of *Nongjiale* on the local environment is underestimated when the female interviewees evaluate their SWB. As was analysed in Section 5.2, the relation between the villagers and *Nongjiale* is still in the euphoria stage – the early stage of tourism development and local perception of tourism impact identified by Doxey (1975). The villagers are attracted and excited by the positive

aspects while neglecting the negative ones at this period of development. However, this does not necessarily mean that environmental problems will not compromise the long-term, rural female well-being. It is reasonable to call attention to the environmental impacts identified and take safeguard actions at the early stage of its appearance.

2. Opportunities of participation in *Nongjiale* are still unequal to all members at the two studied villages. Involvement in *Nongjiale* is relatively low compared to other forms of tourism business operations since to start up a *Nongjiale* business one needs some seed fund. The result is that families with considerable savings seized the chances while those without start-up fund were deprived of the participation opportunities and this inevitably will ultimately lead to the polarization of the rich and the poor in the villages. Equality is one of the key criteria of sustainable development. If rural tourism cannot develop in an equitable way in the villages, it is very likely that it will fail in its positive role of enhancing the overall well-being of the rural females. Therefore, the village committee and the town government should play their role in supporting and ensuring equal participation of *Nongjiale* tourism operation through means of funds, skill trainings and preferential policies to help those low-income and low-education females who have a strong desire to participate in *Nongjiale*.

Conclusion

In the special context of Chinese rural-urban migration, women play a crucial role in the sustainable development of the rural areas. Their stay with their family in the village benefits the health and happiness of the kids and the aged members, and their involvement in *Nongjiale* tourism operations contributes profoundly to the sustainability and vitality of the rural society in China. This justifies the value and meaning of our research, which has taken two villages in the rural outskirts of Jinan city, China, as case studies, and has examined, using a mix of qualitative and quantitative methods, how involvement of *Nongjiale* operations impacts the rural females' life and subjective well-being. It is argued that *Nongjiale* rural tourism turns out to be an effective alternative strategy to sustain the rural females' life and to play a positive role in enhancing their subjective well-being. This research also sheds light on the domain of tourism and rural female well-being which offers rich opportunities of further interdisciplinary research.

REFERENCES

Conceicao, P. and R. Bandura (2014) *Measuring Subjective Well-Being: A Summary Review of the Literature*. New York: Office of Development Studies, United Nations Development Program (UNDP). Retrieved on 25 January 2014 from http://web.undp.org/developmentstudies/docs/subjective_wellbeing_conceicao_bandura.pdf

Diener, E. and E. Suh (1997) 'Measuring Quality of Life: Economic, Social, and Subjective Indicators', *Social Indicators Research*, 40.

Doxey, G.V. (1975) 'A Causation Theory of Visitor-Resident Irritants: Methodology and Research Inferences'. In *Sixth Annual Conference Proceedings*. San Diego: Travel and Tourism Research Associations.

Fan, X., X. Zhen and X. Ding (2007) 'On the Relation between Women and PPT Project', *Journal of China Women's Study*, 19 (6).

Koutsou, S., O. Notta, V. Samathrakis and M. Partalidou (2009) 'Women's Entrepreneurship and Rural Tourism in Greece: Private Enterprises and Cooperatives', *South European Society and Politics*, 14 (2).

Lane, B. (1994) 'What is Rural Tourism?', *Journal of Sustainable Tourism*, 2 (1–2).

Li, F. (2009) 'Land Loss and Job Loss: An Investigation on the Employment of the Land-Loss Farmers in the Process of Urbanization', *Jianghan Tribune*, 2.

Lin, Q. and S. Ding (2009) 'Tourism Development and Women in Host Society: A Gender Analysis', *Collection of Women's Studies*, 93 (3).

Liu, Y. (2007) 'Research of the Effects of Rural Tourism on the Tibetan Women: A Case Study of Jiaju Tibetan Village Scenic Spot of Sichuan Province', *Nationalities Research in Qinghai*, 18 (4).

Markantoni, M. and B. van Hoven (2012) 'Bringing 'Invisible' Side-activities to Light: A Case Study of Rural Female Entrepreneurs in the Veenkoloniën, The Netherlands', *Journal of Rural Studies*, 28.

McGehee, N.G., K. Kim and G.R. Jennings (2006) 'Gender and Motivation for Agri-tourism Entrepreneurship', *Tourism Management*, 28.

McGillivray, M. (2007) Human Well-Being: Issues, Concepts and Measures. In Mark McGillivray (Ed.), *Human Well-Being: Concept and Measurement*. Basingstoke: Palgrave Macmillan.

Organization for Economic Co-operation and Development (OECD) (1994) *Tourism Strategies and Rural Development*. Paris: OECD.

Schimmack, U. (2006) Internal and External Determinants of Subjective Well-Being: Review and Policy Implications. In Y. Kwang Ng and L. Sang Ho (Eds), *Happiness and Public Policy: Theory, Case Studies, and Implications*. Basingstoke: Palgrave Macmillan.

Shao, Q.W. (2007) *Developing Rural Tourism and Promoting the Construction of New Countryside*. Retrieved on 25 January 2014 from http://www.gov.cn/jrzg/2007-01/01/content_485625.htm

Sia, R.J.L., B. Wu, J. Park, H. Shu and A. Morrison (2013) 'Women's Role in Sustaining Villages and Rural Tourism in China', *Annals of Tourism Research*, 43.

Su, B. (2011) 'Rural Tourism in China', *Tourism Management*, 32 (6).

Urry, J. (2002) *The Tourist Gaze*. London: Sage.

Xiying Tourism Office (2013) *Tourism Statistics Database*.

Zhang, Y. (2010) 'A Retrospect of the Research for China's Lost-Land Peasants of the 10 Years', *Journal o f Shanghai University (Social Sciences)*, 17 (5).

Zhao, W., B. Ritchie and C. Echtner (2011) 'Social Capital and Tourism Entrepreneurship', *Annals of Tourism Research*, 38 (4).

Zheng, Y., Z. Zhou and S. Zhu (2012) 'A Review of the Study on Hot Issues in China's Domestic Rural Tourism in the Past Five Years (2007–2011)', *Academic Journal of Beijing International Studies University*, 205 (5).

7

Tribal Cultural Traditions and Women Empowerment in Natural Resource Management

DEBASHIS DEBNATH

The concept of empowerment became very important in the field of development studies during sixties. Nowadays women are the centre of development studies and their empowerment is a crucial issue because gender discrimination and disparities are generating the multiple forms of exploitation in the socio-cultural system. Women empowerment is a burning subject in the present day world, especially in a developing country like India. The meanings of women's empowerment in a nutshell are women's sense of self-worth for their right to have access to opportunities and resources; to control their own lives, both within and outside the home; and to influence the direction of social change nationally and internationally.

A number of incidences of physical violence, mental torture, discrimination in employment opportunities and family disharmony due to hostile attitudes of the in-laws occur every day. The objective of women empowerment is to create an enabling environment where women can freely exercise their rights both within and outside the home as equal partners along with men. The international indices of empowerment of women such as the Gender Empowerment Measures (GEM) developed in the United Nations Development Programme (UNDP) and Human Resources Development (HRD) involve the extent of woman's:

1. Power over economic resources as depicted through per capita income;
2. Access to the professional activities and participation in decision-making based on share of jobs on the professional, technical, managerial and administrative categories; and
3. Political opportunities and decision-making reflected by the share of parliamentary seats.

In Indian Constitution the principle of gender equality provides the first guidelines to empower women and simultaneously to adopt measures of positive discrimination in favour of women. In recent years empowerment has been recognized as the central issue in determining the status of women. The National Commission of Women was setup by an Act of Parliament in 1990 to safeguard the right and legal entitlements of women. The 73rd and 74th Amendments (1993) to the Constitution of India have laid a foundation stone for their participation in decision-making at the local levels. In consequence, Indian women are leading 72,120 village Panchayats, out of total 2,34,676 village Panchayats in India and are representing 36.87 per cent of the 28.18 lakh elected Panchayat representatives (Indiastat.com 2001). India has ratified various international conventions and human right instruments committing to ensure equal rights to women. However, there still exists a wide gap between the goals enunciated in the constitution, legislation, polices, plans, programmes and related mechanism on one hand and the situational reality of the status of women in India on the other. Gender disparity manifests itself in various forms. The most obvious being the trend of continuously declining female ratio in the population, violence against women at the domestic and societal levels, discrimination against girl children and so on. The underlying causes of gender inequality are related to social and economic structure, which is based on informal and formal norms and practices. Consequently, the access of women belonging to weaker sections specially Scheduled Castes and Scheduled

Tribes to development programmes viz. education, health and productive resources is inadequate. Therefore, they remain largely marginalized, poor and socially excluded. The objective of this paper is to discuss the above points through various illustrations from different parts of India.

Women Status in Tribal Culture

In tribal society, women and nature are inseparable from each other as nature is governed by feminine principle – life-supporting, sharing and diversity and the women's support and contribution in upholding the society is immense. In the various studies on the tribal women in India (Mann 1987; Chauhan 1990; Ghosh 1987; Majumdar 1973; Rivers 1973) they are shown as valuable human resources who contribute in domestic, social, cultural and aesthetic life. In tribal societies a woman supports the whole family from dawn to dusk starting from cleaning of house and utensils, fetching water, collection of fuel wood and vegetation, cooking and nurturing children and so on. In their activities they are found as collectors, users, protectors, conservers, sellers and managers of the available resources. Such multi-variant roles always give them a better status in comparison to their non-tribal women counterparts. In the social institutions we find some social liberalization. For instance, there is no child marriage and no stigma on widowhood. She enjoys the right to decide about her marriage etc. Instead of dowry there is bride price indicating high social status of the tribal women. A tribal woman can divorce and marry easily. She earns and is, therefore, to a great extent economically independent. However, there are many facts which indicate a low status for the tribal woman. For example, the tribal women are paid less wage in comparison to the male counterpart for the same work. Several taboos discriminating against tribal women exist in certain tribal groups implying impurity and the low status. The tribal women cannot hold the office of priest. There are taboos related to menstruation as in non-tribal communities. The Kharia women cannot touch a plough nor can she participate in roofing of a house. The Oraon women are also prevented from touching a plough. The Todas of Nilgiri Hills do not touch a menstruating woman for fear of destruction of harvest. In certain tribes only the males can participate in ancestor worship. The Toda and Kota women in

Southern India cannot cross the threshold of a temple. The Santal women cannot attend communal worship. Tribal women do not have property rights except in a matrilineal society, which is small portion of tribal population.

In matrilineal society the descent is traced through female lines, but political power generally rests with men. Land and other property are inherited through women, but its management is done by men (Dube 1990: 97). In Meghalaya there is Khasi saying 'War and politics are for men, while property and children are for women'. Among them, the rulers, chiefs and power-wielding 'elders' are all male, but women have important economic roles.

Rivers (1973), Dalton (1872) and Grigson (1938) have reported low status of women among Todas, Kharias and Maria Gonds with reference to certain taboos during certain periods and ceremonies. Majumdar (1973) has reported a higher status of tribal women on some indicators, while lower on other, while Shasi (1978: 63) has concluded that the status of tribal women varies from tribe to tribe.

The status and position of women is still subordinate due to the patriarchal socio-cultural structure of the society. Existing socio-cultural characteristics like caste, marital status, economic condition, level of education and access to information are the determining factors of the status/position of women in society.

In the context of empowerment, the status of tribal women is reflected in the lower educational status, lower literacy rate, lower enrolment rate and higher drop-outs in the schools. The literacy rate among the tribal females is 34.76 per cent as written in 2001 Census, which is comparatively lesser than general females, that is 53.67 per cent. A very large majority of tribals (almost 90%) are engaged in agriculture; their other economic activities being food gathering (including hunting and fishing), pastoral, handicrafts, trade and commerce, and industrial labour. Rarely are they engaged in one occupation. The employment status of tribal women may be considered in terms of their work participation, agriculture, forests, non-agricultural activities and impact of development programmes. Their work participation is 33 per cent in comparison to males which is 52 per cent. From the comprehensive analysis of the health status of tribal women

(Basu 1993) it has been found that they have higher infant mortality rate, low nutritional status, lower life expectancy and a higher fertility rate.

Still in the modern era the impression of the tribal society in the minds of other people comes from the women sections. Since the earliest form of livelihoods, i.e. gathering-foraging activities, their role and responsibilities are still prominent as found among the Primitive Tribal Groups (PTG), a special category of tribals having pre-agrarian occupation which was so designated in the Fifth Five Year Plan and which has now been categorized as Particularly Vulnerable Tribal Groups (PVTG) in the Tenth Five Year Plan. In the pre-agrarian tribal communities the equity is observed among tribal men and women. In many conservation movements such as Chipko in 1973, the ethos of tribal women are very much prominent and reflected. Further, in the follow-up of National Forest Policy in 1988 the tribal women have been considered as key stakeholders in Participatory Forest Management. Considering their symbiotic relationship, they have been brought in the decision-making process in natural resources management and community development. A number of measures have been adopted to meetup the daily requirement of fuel woods, fodder, Non-timber Forest Products (NTFPs) and medicinal plants. In planning and implementation, their involvement has been emphasized as they face large number of problems. In employment and income generating activities, capacity building and skill development programmes have been organized. In the community mobilization and development the local non-governmental organizations and community-based organizations have taken up significant role. It has been found that formation of Self-Help Groups (SHGs) of tribal women is the best organizational process to generate livelihoods as well as provide equity and sustainability.

Educational Status of Tribal Women

The need for empowerment of tribal women is reflected in the lower educational status, lower literacy rate, lower enrolment rate and higher drop-outs in the schools. The literacy rate of the tribal population as well as Scheduled Castes and general population for three decades (1981–2001) are given in Table 1.

Table 1
Literacy Rates among General Population and Scheduled Tribes (1981–2001)

Category	*General*			*Scheduled Tribes*		
Year	1981	1991	2001	1981	1991	2001
Total	43.57	52.21	64.84	16.35	29.60	47.10
Male	56.38	64.13	75.26	24.52	40.65	59.17
Female	29.76	39.29	53.67	8.04	18.19	34.76

Source: Census of India 1981, 1991 and 2001

Economic Status of Tribal Women

The employment status of tribal women may be considered in terms of their work participation, agriculture, forests, non-agricultural activities and impact of development programmes. Table 2 shows the work participation rates from the period 1981 to 2001.

Table 2
Work Participation Rates 1981–2001

Year	*1981*		*1991*		*2001*	
Section	Male	Female	Male	Female	Male	Female
General	51.6	14.0	51.0	16.0	49.0	19.0
Scheduled Tribes	56.7	28.2	53.7	30.0	52.0	33.0

Source: Census of India 1981, 1991 and 2001

Health Status of Tribal Women

From the comprehensive analysis of the health status of tribal women conducted by Basu (1993) the following traits were found: Higher infant mortality rate; Low nutritional status; Lower life expectancy; Higher fertility rate; High incidence of Sickle-cell disease (HBss) and Glucose-to-Phosphate-Enzyme Deficiency (G-6-80). It is also found that their ill-health is positively related with illiteracy.

Women Empowerment in Joint Forest Management (JFM)

JFM is a collaborative forest management regime for sharing of products, responsibilities, control and decision-making authority over forest lands between forest departments and local user groups based on a formal agreement. In this management regime there is a paradigm shift from centralized, custodial, controlled, timber harvesting and revenue earning forestry to decentralized, participatory community forest management. This process envisaged the involvement of the tribals in protection, management and development of forest in India. Till date all the twenty eight states have declared their JFM resolutions and consequently 1,200,000 JFM communities have been formed which has resultantly brought 17 million hectare of forest areas under JFM activities.

The JFM process started in 1990 with the declaration of resolution at the national level following the forest policies of 1988 which also envisaged women's participation in the protection of forests. The rules of the GOI Order 1991 specified that at least two women should be on every village management committee in the JFM programmes. In 1998, an advisory committee to promote the involvement of women in the forestry sector was constituted by the Ministry of Environment and Forests. It submitted a number of recommendations which would increase women's participation (GOI 1999, cf. Godbole 2002). Following these recommendations it was decided that 50 per cent of the members of the JFM General Body (GB) should be women and the presence of at least 50 per cent of women members should be requisite for calling a GB meeting. Besides the JFM resolution of 2000 has emphasized on 33 per cent representation of women in Executive Committees also. In the official JFM committees in all states, established for the implementation of the programme, there is a provision for compulsory participation of a certain number of women from the concerned communities.

Thus policy has given due consideration to the important role played by tribal women as resource users and has been instrumental in empowering them. JFM can play an important role in achieving the four dimensions of empowerment, i.e.

social empowerment, political empowerment, economic empowerment and psychological empowerment. The following measures needs to be taken for making JFM movement more women friendly:

Providing an Enabling Environment to Realize their Full Potential and Self-worth

In most of the states JFM resolution through the members of Joint Forest Management Committee (JFMC) has been given usufruct rights on Non-timber Forest Products (NTFPs) but in most cases major economically beneficial NTFPs are nationalized as a result of which the JFMC members do not get the full autonomy over the resource in the JFM areas. In most of the areas women are the primary collectors of NTFPs. An effective measure of empowerment is to give them rights to collect, sell and retain the revenues from the sale of all the major NTFPs. In tandem with giving rights to collection of NTFPs from a community managed forest, the government should allow women to sell them in the open market instead of restricting sale to government agencies such as the *Girijan* Cooperative Corporation (Andhra Pradesh). Exclusive rights of collection and processing should be given to the women NTFP collectors and their organizations/SHGs and monopoly leases should be cancelled. These SHGs should be trained in sustainable harvesting of the NTFPs resources and should be levied fines on exploitation or improper maintenance of the resource. The state of Madhya Pradesh has moved in this direction by recently granting ownership rights of NTFPs to tribals. The state should also make provision for storage to primary collectors' organizations on rent.

Women SHG federation should be formed within the JFMCs where women collectors can sell and buy their NTFPs at present rates. Effective institutional platforms of the women NTFP collectors should be established for improved access to finance. The women NTFP collectors should also be given training on value addition and processing techniques so that they can sell the collected NTFPs profitably at a higher value.

In addition to this, species that yield locally preferred NTFPs should be promoted instead of fast-growing varieties. In the long-term this will ease the burden on women to meet both the subsistence and income needs of their households. Women's multiple use of forests is sustainable only with species that yield NTFPs. Fast-growing species that yield timber and construction poles might generate revenues for forest management but will not alleviate the burdens of women.

Providing a Conducive Environment for Enjoyment of All Human Rights and Fundamental Freedom

In the JFM programme the JFMC helps them to develop their potential, ensures freedom of thought, participation in decision-making and working without the feeling of being deprived. Special attention needs to be given to capacity building and education of the women through trainings and awareness generating programmes so that women are aware of their fundamental rights. In JFM meetings equal weightage should be given to women related issues and JFMC should provide them with the opportunity to express their concerns and views.

Disparity in the ownership and control over resources relative to gender responsibilities places women in a subordinate and disempowered position compared to men as they are forever dependent and run a greater risk of being excluded from their homes and livelihood (Sarin et al. 1996). Despite the shortcomings, women are involved and benefiting from various aspects of the programme, particularly in NTFP collection and trade, micro credit, vegetable gardening and forest wage work. In more than 80 per cent of the cases studied by Indian Institute of Forest Management (IIFM), Bhopal, women have been found seemingly active in programme implementation (Singhal et al. 2000).

Equal Access to Participation and Decision-making

The JFM activity begins with formation of village institutions constituted by at least one male and one female member from each household to keep a balance in equitable sharing of responsibility. Women sections suffer maximum due to degradation and depletion of natural resources because they are responsible to meet up the daily requirement of fuel wood, fodder, food, water, etc. Considering their role significant, in many states the women belonging to landless section or backward section are given special status in executive body of the village *Vana Suraksha Samity* (Forest Protection Committee). The mechanisms established by the Forest Department to promote women's involvement need to be further strengthened, particularly with regard to representation for women on the Executive Body. Women's participation needs to be ascertained compulsorily. Hence women members should be involved even in planning process and for that women NGO representatives should be hired on spearhead planning teams for doing so in the whole Participatory Rural Appraisal (PRA) based planning.

Studies reveal during the initial phase of JFM women were consulted through household surveys and interviews, but subsequently their contribution and participation in meetings and decision-making has declined. A study conducted by IIFM in Madhya Pradesh states that though in 70 per cent of the cases women were consulted during PRA, but in only 33 per cent of these they are actively involved in meetings and decision-making. It further reports that in 25 per cent of the cases women complain that they did not have time to attend meetings and so their husbands and children informed them about the groups decisions made in the meetings (Singhal et al. 2000). So, in order to enhance women participation in meetings and planning the venue, time and the date of these meetings should be fixed after consultation with the women members and prior intimation of these meetings should be given so that it is convenient to attend them.

In Jahana village, Ranchi district of Jharkhand in the Forest Protection Committee is an all women team. In the bio-diversity conservation women's knowledge of species diversity among trees, shrubs and herbs are valuable. In resource mapping women's involvement have been strengthened to assess the resource potentiality with variability of species. As part of the learning environment, significant changes in practice to broaden participation in Forest Committees have been put in place. For example development of self-help groups that target women's participation has increased in leaps and bounds over the years. The Government Resolution has been amended twice to reflect the need for greater representation by women and also by Non-Government Organizations (NGOs).

Another important contribution (although again difficult to quantify) that women can make to forest improvement is through their knowledge of how certain forest products should be extracted when the forest is opened periodically, or which products to promote in planting efforts. Their knowledge about the products that they typically collect and which require particular skills, such as how tree fodder should be plucked (excessive plucking can reduce growth) and at what stage of its development – some fodder leaves are best when young, others are poisonous when young (Carter 1992: 55) – or how ground grass should be cut, or medicinal herbs and wild vegetables procured, can also prove significant in forest conservation efforts.

Changing Social Attitudes and Community Practices

A gender perspective can uncover patterns of resource control with implications for refining JFM policy. For example, in a study of women and forests in Jharkhand, it was observed that women play an important role in gathering forest produce. Within the family the income from sale of forest produce tends to be counted as the income of the individual who gathers and sells the produce. Increasing the income from forestry will thus also help strengthen the position of women within the family. Here is an instance where women have the same rights as men vis-à-vis control of income from the sale of forest products. JFM policy initiatives, to begin with, should capitalize on such gender equal opportunities, wherever they are present, to improve the social, and economic standing of women.

With the implementation of Panchayat Extension in Scheduled Area (PESA) 1996, the quorum of the gram sabha is formed with the presence of 50 per cent of the women members. In the JFM committees the guidelines have been followed in the tribal states like Jharkhand, Madhya Pradesh, Chhattisgarh with 33 per cent reservation for the women in village institution and 30 per cent reservation for women in heading the village committees.

Mainstreaming a Gender Perspective in the Development Process

In the JFM programme financial support has been given for the upbringing of girl children and subsidiary food support is provided to the pregnant and lactating mothers for nutrition. In the villages of Harda district, in Madhya Pradesh, it was found that under *Vatsalya Yojana* ₹ 500 was given from Block Development Office to households for bringing up their girl children while pregnant and lactating mothers were provided *dalia* (cereal) for nutrition under Integrated Child Development Scheme (ICDS) project.

Building and Strengthening Partnerships with Civil Society, Particularly Women's Organizations

JFM is itself partnership based community forest management enlarging the collaboration of not only village people and Forest Department, but also a number of stakeholders which are informal groups and formal organizations. We find that a number of civil society organizations and community-based organizations play an important role and responsibility here. Among these, women's organizations like Women Studies Centre in Barkatullah University, *Mahila Chetana Kendra*, Bhopal and informal women groups like *Mahila Mandal* in Chhattisgarh and *Bairani Kuldis* in Jhabua in Madhya Pradesh may be mentioned. Women's self-help group (SHG) is one of the successful indicators of women empowerment. These SHGs have been working effectively in poverty reduction and environmental management. Through SHG the women get employment in nursery raising, seed storing, pitdigging, plantation, water harvesting structures and so on. In many divisions, Madhya Pradesh Forest Department (MPFD) staff has introduced women's self-help savings groups to provide a venue and focus for women's involvement (there are about 2000 such SHGs). This has resulted in their participation in these savings group activities but rarely are the links built back to the aims of forest management. The MPFD recognizes the weaknesses in women's involvement in the programme and is trying to address this through local training for staff, village leaders and women's groups; through collaboration with NGOs and in promoting leadership within the villages of more educated women but a great deal of work still is required to this end.

In Vellore forest division of Tamil Nadu under Tamil Nadu Afforestation Programme (TAP), a JFM programme funded by Japan Bank of International Cooperation (JBIC) was started in which a number of local NGOs started to develop the capacity of women SHGs to produce vermi-compost as non-chemical organic fertilizers were used for raising medicinal plants in the community and forest lands. To mobilize the people along with the confidence building, the Forest Department organized various training programmes for the women SHGs in alternative economic sources for the income generation with the help of local NGOs and some skill development units of the line department, which are involved in livelihood interventions. These alternative economic pursuits are candle making, plastic bag making, tailoring, etc. Some SHGs were also encouraged to produce guava in the leased land and many women SHGs raised *Kasinikeeri* (Chchorium sp.) in their agricultural fields, which they marketed to raise their income level (Debnath 2005).

Some Constraints Faced in Women's Participation in JFM

Agarwal (2010) has identified the following obstacles for women's participation in JFM activities:

i. Membership criteria defining who can join the GB and EC: In most of the states only one member of the household can be the member of the EC or GB and in such a case the male persons become the member. In Madhya Pradesh two members of a household can become the members.
ii. Social norms that define women's appropriate roles and behaviour in states where membership is not an obstacle, the social norms can still be a major hindrance to women's participation in many ways. Rural women are generally over-burned with household work, childcare, NTFP collection, fuel wood collection in addition to their share of agricultural work and cattle care. Due to these workloads women do not get the time to participate in lengthy JFM meetings which are generally held at inconvenient timings. Gendered behavioural norms also create subtle

hierarchies. In most of the meetings women members avoid sitting in the front or when senior members are present at the meetings they hesitate to attend meetings or speaking up in front of them or opposing men publicly. The hierarchy that marks respectful family behaviour thus carries over into community spaces.

iii. Social perceptions regarding women's abilities: In most cases it has been observed that women's involvement in the JFM meetings have always been considered unuseful by men who tend to downplay their potential contribution. Women have been included in the EC only because of the forest department's intervention.

iv. The culture of public discourse: The aggressive culture of public interaction in male dominated forums is another reason why women do not attend meetings saying that they feel threatened by men's behaviour.

v. Personal endowments and attributes (e.g. women's education levels, property status, age, etc.): The fact that rural women typically lack personal property such as land and are seldom well connected politically reduces the weight of their opinions and their limited experience of interaction in public forums undermines their effectiveness.

Women's Self-Help Groups (SHGs)

Women's SHG is one of the successful indicators of women empowerment. These SHGs have been working effectively in poverty reduction and environmental management.

Two Case Studies on SHG

Social Entrepreneurship

In a study of Jhabua district in Madhya Pradesh the author noted down the alternative livelihoods generation. A successful case of micro-enterprise was observed in the village Kajailidungri. About 15 women members of the saving groups got united to form a Women's Co-operative called 'Amruit Mahila Audhyogik Co-operative Ltd'. This society is the major stakeholder of the entrepreneurship development project and produces blended nutritious food or complementary food, which is supplied to the ICDS projects in the district. The project is funded under the World Food Programme and assisted by NGO. Similarly in the village Goraikhadan, ten women formed a SHG, each contributing ₹ 10 per month. Later they obtained bank loans twice of ₹ 5,000 and ₹ 25,200. This fund helped the members in purchasing agricultural equipments, investing in cultivation, children's education, repayment of loan to private moneylenders, saving them from undue exploitation, milk dairy, etc. (Debnath 2002).

Case of Lashmi Swa-Sahayata Samuh, Katangudih Forest Protection Committee, Raighar Division

Chhattisgarh is one of the youngest states of the Indian nation and was formerly a part of Madhya Pradesh. The state of Chhattisgarh being placed in Deccan bio-geographical area, houses an important part of that rich and unique biological diversity. The state is significantly rich in endemism with respect to many plants having medicinal importance. The forests of the state fall under two major forest types, i.e. tropical moist deciduous forests and the tropical dry deciduous forests. The state of Chhattisgarh is endowed with about 22 varied sub-types. The Forest Policy of Chhattisgarh, 2001 clearly lays down the importance of people's involvement in administering the forest areas. Necessary provisions have been made for the adequate participation at all levels of decision-making by the landless, marginal farmers and women in all JFM bodies like Village Forest Committee (VFC), Forest Protection Committee (FPC) and Eco Development Committee (EDC). There are two types of JFM committee in the state. One Forest Protection Committee (FPC) and the other is Village Forest Committee (VFC). FPCs are formed in those villages, which are adjoining to dense forests. The VFCs are formed in those villages, which are adjoining to degraded forests. There are 6,953 FPC/VFC committees in the state. The break up is given in Table 3.

Table 4 gives details of Women Self-Help Groups formed under JFM Programme in the state of Chhattisgarh.

Table 3

No. of FPCs and VFCs in JFMC of Chhattisgarh

FPC	*VFC*	*Total*	*Male*	*Female*	*Total Scheduled Tribe Household*	*Total Members*
3,547	3,406	6,953	7,88,789	6,37,883	2,07,923	14,26,672

Note: FPC – Forest Protection Committee, VFC – Village Forest Committee and JFMC – Joint Forest Management Committee

Table 4

Women Self-Help Groups in JFM in Chhattisgarh

Name of Circle	*FPC/ VFC*	*No. of SHGs*	*No of Beneficiaries*	*Total Amount (₹)*	*Amount Granted for Loan*
Raipur	1,214	377	8,475	1,38,624	3,64,880
Durg	731	50	1,209	54,627	3000
Bilaspur	1,287	232	5,869	3,81,382	4,67,565
Jagdalpur	7,058	05	60	0	0
Kanker	937	29	617	4,041	800
Sarguja	2,121	63	1,095	39,096	5,400
Total	13,348	756	17,325	36,15,761	8,41,645

As case was developed in the Raigarh division of Chhattisgarh. Forty one SHGs have been formed in which total number of beneficiaries are 1,023, total amount deposited is ₹ 9,01,289 and the amount of the loan is ₹ 2,16,388.53 (See Table 5). The above-mentioned SHGs as shown in Table 5 were formed in 1999 with the support of Forest Department. Total number of SHG members is 15. Every week the committee meeting was held. An amount of ₹ 20 per month per member was deposited in the Rural Regional Bank. The SHG took land on lease from its savings, which they used for paddy cultivation and in the last 3 years since 2005 they have earned ₹ 16,000 from paddy cultivation. Now they have purchased land in the name of SHG. In the year 2002–03 they undertook bamboo plantation which cost around ₹ 3,000. They sold the bamboo plants to Marwahi Forest Division and got ₹ 35,000 as income and total profit was ₹ 32,000. In the year 2008 the expected income from bamboo plantation was ₹ 40,000.

Table 5

No. of SHGs and Beneficiaries in the Raigarh Forest Division

Name of the Division	*No. of SHGs Formed*	*Total No. of Beneficiaries*	*Total Amount Deposited*	*Amount Given Loan*
Raigarh	41	1,023	90,1289.00	2,16,388.53

Grass for aromatic oil and *amla* have been planted on the SHG land. So, now they have ₹ 12,846 in the SHG's savings account and ₹ 1,50,000 as fixed deposit. The initiative taken by SHGs for income generation and training has been provided for skill development in the following livelihood options mentioned in Table 6.

Table 6

Livelihood Option with Number of SHG Members

S.No.	*Livelihood Option*	*No. of SHG Members*
1	Incense sticks machine	08
2	Dona pattal machine	12
3	Broom making	13
4	Husking pad making	13
5	Spices manufacturing	14
6	Medicinal packing machine	11
7	Bottle sealing machine	11
8	Papad manufacturing	11
9	Lac cultivation	13
10	Sericulture	14
11	Mat and rope making	05
12	Bee culture	06
13	Sabai rope making	11

Conclusion

In tribal society, women and nature are inseparable from each other as nature is governed by feminine principle – life-supporting, sharing and diversity and the women's support and contribution in upholding the society are immense. In pre-agrarian tribal communities equity is observed among tribal men and women. Various ethnographic studies have found several cultural norms which show the high status of tribal women. In various movements the conservation ethos of tribal women are very much prominent and reflected. The 1973 Chipko movement is a great illustration. Following the National Forest Policy of 1988 and 1990 on JFM resolution of Ministry of Environment and Forests, Government of India, the tribal women have been considered as key stakeholder in Participatory Forest Management. Considering their symbiotic relationship they have been brought in the decision-making process in natural resources management and community development. A number of measures have been adopted to meet up the daily requirement of fuelwoods, fodder, NTFPs and medicinal plants. In the planning and implementation their involvement has been emphasized as they face a large number of problems. In the direction of employment and income generating activities, capacity building and skill development programmes have been organized. In the community mobilization the local non-governmental organizations and community-based organizations have taken up a significant role. It has been found that formation of Self-Help Groups (SHGs) of tribal women is the best organizational process to generate livelihoods as well as provide equity and sustainability.

REFERENCES

Agarwal, Bina (2010) *Gender and Green Governance: The Political Economy of Women's Presence Within and Beyond Community Forestry*. New Delhi: Oxford University Press.

Basu, S.K. (1993) *Study on Fertility and Mortality Trends among Bal Population of India: A Review*. New Delhi: Indian Council of Social Science Research.

Carter, J.E. (1992) 'Tree Cultivation on Private Land in Nepal's Middle Hills: An Investigation into Local Knowledge and Local Needs', *Oxford Forestry Institute Occasional Papers*, No. 40.

Chauhan, Abha (1990) *Tribal Women and Social Change in India*. Etawah: A.C. Brothers.

Dalton, E.T. (1872) *Descriptive Ethnography of Bengal*. Calcutta: Government of West Bengal Press.

Debnath, D. (2002) 'Jhabua Watershed Development Project: An Overview', *IIFM Newsletter*, V (3), September issue.

—— (2005) 'Conservation, Cultivation of Medicinal Plants in Livelihood Intervention: A Case Study of Tamil Nadu', *IIFM Communiqué* (A Newsletter of IIFM), VII, March issue.

Dube, S.C. (1990) *Indian Society*. New Delhi: National Book Trust.

Ghosh, S. (1987) 'Women's Role in Health and Development', *Health for the Millions*, XIII (1 and 2).

Godbole, Girija (2002) 'Joint Forest Management and Gender', *Working Paper*, September.

Grigson, W.V. (1938) *The Maria Gonds of Bastar*. Oxford: Oxford University Press.

Indiastat.com (2001) Statewise Number of Elected Women Members in Panchayati Raj in India. Retrieved from www.indiastat.com on 1 August 2013.

Majumdar, D.N. (1973) *A Glimpse of Garo Politics in North-Eastern Affairs*. London: Longman.

Mann, K. (1987) *Tribal Women in Changing Society*. Delhi: Mittal Publications.

Rivers, H.H. (1973) *The Todas*. London: Macmillan.

Sarin, M. et al. (1996) 'From Conflict to Collaboration: Local Institution in Joint Forest Management', *JFM Working Paper*, No. 14. New Delhi: SPWD and The Ford Foundation.

Shasi, S.S. (1978) *The Tribal Women of India*. New Delhi: Sandeep Prakashan.

Singhal, R. et al. (2000) *Process Documentation of Joint Forest Management and Eco-development: Consultancy Report*. Bhopal: Indian Institute of Forest Management for Madhya Pradesh Forestry Project.

8

Empowering Tribal Women through Livelihood Opportunity

A Study of Odisha (India)

CHINMAYEE SATPATHY

Livelihood is defined as a set of activities, involving securing water, food, fodder, medicine, shelter, clothing and the capacity to acquire above necessities working either individually or as a group by using endowments (both human and material) for meeting the requirements of the self and his/her household on a sustainable basis with dignity. Livelihood comprises the capabilities, assets (including both material and social resources) and activities required for acquiring means of living. A livelihood is sustainable when it can cope with and recover from stress and shocks and maintain or enhance its capabilities and assets both now and in the future, while not undermining the natural resource base (Chambers and Conway 1992).

The tribal communities are the original inhabitants of the land representing around 8 per cent of Indian population. Not only are they crucial components of the country's human biodiversity, but also are important sources of economic and socio-cultural heritage. Indigenous communities, especially women, are the custodians of traditional wisdom and culture, natural resource management, waste management, medicine, metallurgy and significantly contribute to the cultural diversity, utilizing human resources and maintaining environmental sustainability. However, industrialization and globalization has posed harmful effects which have drastically changed the tribal life. In the socio-political and economic struggle and in the process of development, tribal women have become the major victims. The launch of mega development projects in the tribal areas has have not only caused irreparable damage to their forest-based subsistent economy but also deprived them of their traditional customary rights and privileges which they and their ancestors were enjoying for generations.

The state of Odisha occupies a unique place in the tribal map of India. It is the second largest tribal dominated state in the country comprising 62 tribal groups that constitute around 22 per cent of total population of the state. Around 73 per cent of tribes live below the poverty line. In Odisha the Scheduled Areas cover 44.71 per cent which includes 118 blocks in 12 districts. The tribal literacy rate of the state is only 37 per cent whereas the tribal female literacy rate is even lower, i.e. 23 per cent (Census of India 2011). Tribes of Odisha are known as *Adivasi* (aborigine), *Vanabasi* (forest dweller) and *Girijana* (mountain dweller). Based upon the level of development, Government of India has classified and declared certain tribal groups as Particularly Vulnerable Tribal Groups (PVTGs) often called Primitive Tribal Groups (PTGs) who are the most backward indigenous ethnic groups. These PVTGs are not only techno-economically backward but are also relatively less acculturated, characterized by declining or stagnant population, low levels of literacy, pre-agricultural technology and primarily belong to the hunting and gathering communities.

Tribal economy in Odisha is subsistence oriented. It shows wide variation in economic pursuits which are generally influenced by ecological characteristics of their habitat and own culture and tradition. Based on the traditional economy, the tribes of Odisha may be grouped under (a) hunters and food gatherers, (b) cattle herders, (c) simple artisans, (d) shifting cultivators, (e) settled agriculturists and (f) industrial workers. Tribal economy still revolves round agriculture in some form or another and continues to be the mainstay of the people as about 90 per cent of their main workers have returned as cultivators and agricultural labourers (SCSTRTI 2004).

Research Works Done in International Context

The term 'feminization of poverty' is frequently used in discussions on the effects of changes in global economic policies on women. The concept is in its initial usage and relatively simple that women and female-headed households tend to be disproportionately represented among the world's poor economies. However, it is used to illustrate the links between social and economic subordination of women. The increase in women's employment does not necessarily lead to poverty reduction and increased household welfare. In other words, women's entry into waged labour is not enough to draw conclusion about the impact on poverty nor does it tell us about the changes in women's economic, social and political position in relation to men. These depend not only on the quantum of women's earnings but the degree to which women control their own income and the manner in which it is spent. It is now more widely accepted that household organization and gender relations are critical variables in livelihood system (Menon-Sen 2001). In some parts of the world, women have almost total control over their own income (for example, in parts of West Africa). In others, their income is handed over to men or to older women (parts of South Asia). The relationship between women's income and their bargaining power is complex, changing and mediated by processes outside as well as inside the household. There is considerable body of research which indicates that women and men have different spending priorities (Bruce and Dwyer 1988; Kanji 1995; Narayan 2000). Women tend to emphasize on food and basic goods for household consumption, while men tend to prioritize items for personal use or investment, rather than household maintenance. In contexts where men hold the purse strings and do not necessarily prioritize basic household needs, has resulted in deterioration in children's nutritional status (Evans 1997). A multi-country study found that the resources (cash and food produce) under the mother's (rather than the father's) control constitute the most important factor in determining the livelihood status in low-income households (Blumberg 1991).

The women workers continue to be primarily responsible for reproductive and domestic work, which is perceived to be their primary function. This perception reinforces structural barriers that prevent women from accessing education, training, land and productive assets. Women's double workload also restricts their time and mobility for productive work, and limits their choices of income-earning activities. Women are perceived to be 'secondary' earners so men often have priority over women in the allocation of opportunities for paid employment. Women do not have equal access to productive resources and services. Because they are largely dependent on self-employment for which land, capital, technology and labour are critical, lack of access constrains their productivity and reinforces the stereotype that they are inherently less productive than men (Menon-Sen 2001).

The women's increased involvement in paid work has not significantly reduced poor women's share of unpaid work in caring for households. Women's gender-ascribed 'caring' roles, the costs of raising children, the existence of social support structures which women can depend on and mechanisms to protect vulnerable groups all affect the extent to which women can enter and participate in the labour market. Along with this decreased social provisioning by the state, liberalization and privatization have shifted the costs of social reproduction from the paid to the unpaid economy, with evidence of negative consequences for women's health and well being and for household welfare in successive generations. When women work for meagre incomes, girls may be taken out of school to help with household work, decreasing their opportunity to acquire marketable skills and increasing their chances of being poor in the future (Elson 1995; Kanji 1995; Moser 1996).

The idea of sustainable livelihoods was first introduced by the Brundtland Commission on Environment and Development as a way of linking socio-economic and ecological considerations in a cohesive, policy-relevant structure. The 1992 United Nations Conference on Environment and Development (UNCED) expanded the concept, especially in the context of Agenda 21, and advocated for the achievement of sustainable livelihoods as a broad goal for poverty eradication. It stated that sustainable livelihoods could serve as 'an integrating factor that allows policies to address 'development, sustainable resource management, and poverty eradication simultaneously (UNDP 1999).

Four types of capital are identified by the Institute for Development Studies (IDS, UK) (which does not seem to be an exhaustive list): Natural capital – the natural resource stocks (soil, water, air, genetic resources, etc.) and environmental services (hydrological cycle, pollution sinks, etc.) from which resource flows and services useful for livelihoods are derived. Economic or financial capital – the capital base (cash, credit/debit, savings, and other economic assets, including basic infrastructure and production equipment and technologies) which is essential for the pursuit of any livelihood strategy. Human capital – the skills, knowledge, ability to labour and good health and physical capability are important for the successful pursuit of different livelihood strategies. Social capital – the social resources (networks, social claims, social relations, affiliations, associations) upon which people draw when pursuing different livelihood strategies requiring co-ordinated actions (Krantz 2001).

Research Works Done in Indian Context

A tribal woman plays a key role in the well-being of the family. Her average contribution in the family income is about 40 per cent in addition to the household activity, which is not treated as economic activity. Generally, the tribal families possess very limited cultivated land, which is undulated and degraded. With hard work, the tribal family tries to get substantial return. In case of wage earning, the woman has to work hard during the day and attend the domestic responsibilities. The contribution of tribal women for the family prosperity is significant and in the present era, her role for the family food security is important as she rarely spends any money for her personal requirements, except for clothes or some customary ornaments purchased at fairs. Her contribution towards the family prosperity is significant where food security is the most important aspect. In totality, the contribution of tribal women in the family earning including activities not treated as economic, is more than half in comparison to male, in real terms. In general tribal family women play a pivotal role in food security.

The study by Awais, Alam and Asif (2009) reviews the emerging perspective in the context of the socio-economic empowerment of tribal women and changing paradigms of development. Even after industrialization and resultant commercialization that swamped the tribal economy, women continued to play a significant role. Collection of minor forest produce is done mostly by women and children. Many also work as labourers in industries, households and construction, contributing to their family income. Despite exploitation by the contractors and managers, the tribal are more sincere and honest than the non-tribal. However, tribal women face problems and challenges in getting a sustainable livelihood and a decent life. The strategy for tribal development, and specially women, needs improvement, betterment, development and upliftment to affect their empowerment. Undoubtedly, the programme oriented towards the empowerment of tribal, particularly women have improved their socio-economic conditions and status. However, there are wide variations across regions and tribes in terms of work participation, sex ratio, economic productivity and social life. The impact of development planning needs to be evaluated in terms of desired and unanticipated consequences.

In a research study on 'Migration of Tribal Women: Its Socio-economic Effects – An In-depth Study of Chhattisgarh, Jharkhand, M.P. and Orissa' it has been observed that a large number of educated, uneducated and illiterate tribal women from Jharkhand, Chhattisgarh, Odisha and West Bengal have migrated to different parts of the country in search of gainful employment/casual labour in the unorganized sector and as household maids for their livelihood. The main cause of migration is that the tribal families are not able to meet their basic needs out of their meagre income from their occupations and are heavily indebted to the moneylenders. They are pledging their fixed assets like land, *mahua* and tamarind trees and mobile articles for meeting their daily expenses and occasional functions. There is no proper marketing and forward and backward linkages of the forest produces and articles which are being produced by the tribes in the rural interior areas. Tribal migrant women exploitation is mostly done by the middlemen who offer them good emoluments, good placement and work conditions and after they are taken to the workplace they are cheated. It has been noticed that they are often exploited physically and sexually (Society for Regional Research and Analysis 2010).

Research Objectives

1. To study the present livelihood status of tribal women in Mayurbhanj district of Odisha relating to the availability of food, safe drinking water, housing, primary health and educational facilities and the extent of utilization of such services by them;
2. To analyse tribal women's accessibility and control over resources available through livelihood programmes and participation in decision-making processes and to address the major challenges faced by them;
3. To explore various livelihood improvement programmes undertaken by different agencies like National Bank for Agriculture and Rural Development (NABARD), banks, cooperatives, Integrated Tribal Development Agency (ITDA), and government and non-government organizations and policy measures adopted to promote livelihood status of tribal women community;
4. To make a note of the practices that make livelihood programmes successful and to formulate development strategy suggesting requisite measures to be adopted for effective mobilization of resources available for retaining the livelihood status of tribal women community.

Research Design and Methods

The study covers Mayurbhanj district, a scheduled district located in the northern part of Odisha. The socio-economic profiles of tribal of Mayurbhanj district show a very complex picture. The major tribes of the district include Santal, Bhumija, Kolha, Bhuyan, Bathudi, Gond and Munda, etc. These tribal groups mostly depend upon agriculture and forest. There are three PVTGs, the Hill Kharia, Mankerdia and Lodha who are mostly landless and depend upon collection of minor forest produces. Selected livelihood indicators such as availability of food, safe drinking water, housing, education facilities and primary healthcare facilities, community resource utilization, use of essential resources, energy use, environment and sanitation are used to assess the present socio-economic profiles of tribal women communities in respect to their health, education, economic opportunities, access and control over resources and participation in decision-making processes.

Stratified random sampling method was used by systematically taking district, block, panchayat, household and women member as 1st, 2nd, 3rd 4th and 5th stage of sampling units. Keeping in view the block wise distribution of tribal population, the blocks are chosen for conducting field-based research study. Two types of interview schedules were used to get relevant information from two broad categories of respondents, tribal women as well as opinions of the experts like bankers, government officials, non-government organizations (NGOs), community leaders, academia, researchers and experts regarding necessary changes required to improve the livelihood situation of tribal women communities. The sources of primary data include household survey, semi-structured informal interview schedule, focus group discussion, case study and observation with the key stakeholders like community leaders, PRIs, government officials, activists, local NGOs, community-based organizations (CBOs) and field-based observations. Besides, the researcher has collected relevant literature from different books and journals and reports and relevant web sources. The quantitative and qualitative data received from different sources are integrated to make the research analysis meaningful and comprehensive.

Research Findings

So far as the present livelihood status of the tribal womenfolk of the Mayurbhanj district is concerned, it shows a very complex picture as they have different literacy rate, population growth and density and several other distinctive features of their own. Regional variation is also noticed as they are at different stages of social and economic development. Besides, these tribal communities are different in their skills, aptitudes, habits, cultures, traditions and customs which have differential impacts on their development as a whole. The PVTGs are at the lowest rung of socio-economic ladder and need special attention for their rehabilitation and development. However, the most common distinctive feature of the PVTGs is that they are socially, educationally and economically backward and isolated from the mainstay of development. The present study shows that different tribal groups have differential access to the basic livelihood necessities such as food, safe drinking water, housing, primary healthcare and education facilities, community resource utilization, use of essential services, energy use, environment and sanitation, etc.

$$\text{Mean score} = \frac{\text{Summation of all scores obtained by all respondents for a particular element}}{\text{Total number of respondents}}$$

Keeping in view of the above distinctive pictures, Table 1 shows the present livelihood system of tribal women in the area of study. It illustrates the extent of availability of the livelihood elements to the women of four different tribal groups, i.e. Santal, Kolha, Hill Kharia and Mankerdia. The livelihood system of the women of the four tribal groups was measured by using 10 important elements cited in the Table 1. The scoring method was followed using a 3 point scale consisting of very much, much and little to which 3, 2 and 1 score were assigned respectively. Thus the mean score was calculated for ten elements of the four tribes.

Table 1

Perceived Present Livelihood System of the Sample Tribes of Mayurbhanj District in Odisha

S. No.	*Elements of Livelihood System*	*Santal*	*Kolha*	*Hill Kharia*	*Mankerdia*
1	Food availability	2.00	2.00	1.86	1.20
2	Safe drinking water	2.15	1.95	1.50	1.10
3	Housing	2.60	2.55	1.56	0.90
4	Primary health care	2.45	2.32	1.64	1.34

Cont'd...

...Cont'd

5	Educational facilities	2.70	2.74	2.15	1.24
6	Community resource utilization	2.40	2.56	2.20	1.40
7	Use of essential services	2.55	2.43	2.11	1.65
8	Energy use	2.87	2.76	2.12	0.54
9	Environment	1.65	1.70	1.87	1.83
10	Sanitation	1.93	1.81	1.78	0.76
11	Average	2.33	2.28	1.87	1.19
12	Gap (%)	41.75	43.00	53.25	70.25

Source: Primary data

While analysing various livelihood elements of women of four tribal groups it was observed that, the availability of food was a concern for both the Santal women and Kolha women who had similar score, i.e. 2.00 while the score obtained by the Hill Kharia women and the Mankerdia women were 1.86 and 1.20 respectively. While examining the availability of safe drinking water, the score obtained by the Santal women was 2.15 and that of Kolha women was 1.95 who were in a better position, in comparison to the Hill Kharia women who got 1.50 score and the Mankerdia women got 1.10 score. Similarly, in getting housing facility, the score obtained by the Santal women was 2.60 and that of Kolha women was 2.55. While comparing the scores of the other two tribes the Hill Kharia women got 1.56 score and so also the Mankerdia women got 0.90 score respectively.

While examining the availability of primary health care facility, Santal women and Kolha women attained 2.45 and 2.32 as scores respectively while the Hill Kharia women got a score of 1.64 and Mankerdia women scored 1.34 in availing the same. In availing educational facility the Kolha women were ahead by obtaining 2.74 score. The score of Santal women was 2.70, that of Hill Kharia women was 2.15 and for Mankerdia women the score was 1.24. Similarly in utilizing community resources, the Kolha women were at the top scoring 2.56 whereas the Santal women obtained 2.40 score and the Hill Kharia women and the Mankerdia women lagged behind obtaining 2.20 and 1.40

scores respectively. In using essential resources, the score obtained by the Santal women was 2.55, and that of Kolha women was 2.43 and in case of Hill Kharia women and Mankerdia women the scores were 2.11 and 1.65 respectively. Similarly in energy use, the Santal women availed 2.87 score and Kolha women availed 2.76 score but in case of Hill Kharia women and Mankerdia women the scores were low at 2.12 and 0.54 respectively. In using environmental resources, the scores obtained by the four tribes varied to a limited extent, i.e. Santal women and Kolha women availed 1.65 score and 1.70 score, while the Hill Kharia women and Mankerdia women availed 1.87 and 1.83 scores respectively. Similarly, in availing sanitation facility, the score obtained by Santal women was 1.93 and that of Kolha women was 1.81, whereas the scores of Hill Kharia women and Mankerdia women were 1.78 and 0.76 respectively. On an average, the Santal women availed 2.33 score, Kolha women availed 2.28 score, Hill Kharia women availed 1.87 score and Mankerdia women availed 1.19 score. Hence, it is evident that the gap was more in case of Hill Kharia women and Mankerdia women which was 53.25 score and 70.25 score respectively whereas the gaps were comparatively less for Santal women and Kolha women which were 41.75 and 43.00 respectively.

From the Table 1 it can be concluded that, the womenfolk of the Santal and Kolha tribe were relatively in a better position in comparison to the womenfolk of the two PVTGs – Hill Kharia and Mankerdia tribe in availing the basic livelihood opportunities. Majority of the tribal women among the PVTGs were not in a position to avail primary healthcare and educational facilities. They suffer from ill-health and are illiterate which affected their livelihood to a considerable extent.

In addition to this, it is also essential to know the access and control of tribal women over various resources and their level of participation in the decision-making process. Table 2 illustrates the sample tribal women's accessibility and control over resources in various livelihood programmes as well as their participation in the decision-making processes.

Table 2
Sample Women's Accessibility and Control over Resources and Participation in Decision-making Process

S. No.	Livelihood Resources	Santal	Kolha	Hill Kharia	Mankerdia
1	Accessibility over resources	3.65	3.35	3.00	2.56
2	Control over resources	3.00	2.98	2.85	2.12
3	Livelihood programmes	2.91	2.90	2.85	2.13
4	Decision-making process	2.50	2.43	2.40	2.20
5	Average	3.01	2.91	2.77	2.25
6	Gaps (%)	24.75	27.25	30.75	43.75

Source: Primary data

The qualitative responses of the tribal women respondents were quantified by assigning the numerals in order to calculate the mean average score. This process was followed for the tribal womenfolk of all the four tribes. The scoring pattern for all the four elements like tribal women's accessibility over resources, control over resources, livelihood programmes and participation in the decision-making process were measured by using a four point scale consisting of very much, much, to some extent and little by assigning them scores of 4,3,2 and 1 respectively. However, the zero scoring was not included because none was isolated in case of all the four elements.

While measuring the accessibility of the women tribal communities to various livelihood resources it was observed that the Santal women scored 3.65, the Kolha women scored 3.35, the Hill Kharia women scored 3.00 and the Mankerdia women scored 2.56. Similarly, while exploring the control of tribal women over various resources, the women from Santal and Kolha communities were in a better position scoring 3.00 and 2.98 respectively, whereas the score of Hill Kharia women was 2.85 and that of Mankerdia women was 2.12 which were comparatively less. Similarly, in availing the facilities of different livelihood programmes, the scores obtained by the Santal women and Kolha women slightly varied with 2.91 and 2.90 as their scores. But in case of Hill Kharia and Mankerdia women the scores were 2.85 and 2.13 respectively. While considering the participation of tribal women in the decision-making process, the

Santal women scored 2.50, and the Kolha women scored 2.43, while the scores of Hill Kharia and Mankerdia women were 2.40 and 2.20 respectively. On an average, the score obtained by the Santal women and Kolha women were 3.01 and 2.91 respectively and that of Hill Kharia women and Mankerdia women were 2.77 and 2.25 respectively. Hence, the gap was more in case of Hill Kharia women and Mankerdia women whose scores were 30.75 and 43.75 respectively whereas the gap was comparatively less in case of Santal women and Kolha women whose score were 24.75 and 27.25 respectively.

Conclusively, it is observed that the sampled women among developing tribes like Santal and Kolha have comparatively more access and control over resources and derive more benefits from various livelihood programmes. The Hill Kharia and Mankerdia tribes on the other hand have less access and control over livelihood resources and get fewer benefits available through various livelihood programmes. The Mankerida women were the most vulnerable when a comparison is made with women from the other categories. So far as participation of the sampled tribal women in the decision-making processes is concerned the representation of Santal and Kolha women were relatively more in comparison to the Hill Kharia and Mankerdia women.

It has been observed from the study that agriculture provides food to the tribal household for a maximum period of six months in a year due to poor productivity and relatively small landholdings. Besides, the livelihood of the tribes is also closely linked with the forest. The PVTGs mainly depend upon the collection of minor forest products to earn their livelihood. Many of them are nomadic and semi-nomadic wandering bands who migrate from one place to another due to exhaustion of resources. But, the new forest policy of government has restricted them from entering into the forest which is a major setback for continuation of their forest-based livelihood. In the absence of any suitable livelihood alternative it becomes increasingly difficult day by day to sustain their livelihood for maintenance of their family. Besides, increasing deforestation due to rapid industrialization has intensified the vulnerability, exploitation and land alienation of these tribal communities. Tribal women suffer to a larger extent in comparison to tribal men as they are mostly involved in household management. The present situation of tribal women is caused mainly due to their ignorance, illiteracy and lack of exposure to the outside world. Besides, the uneven distribution patterns of resources, infrastructure, wealth, knowledge and non-utilization of such services have affected the livelihood status of tribal household to a significant extent. In recent years various livelihood improvement programmes undertaken by different agencies like National Bank for Agriculture and Rural Development (NABARD), State Cooperatives, Integrated Tribal Development Agencies (ITDA), and non-government organizations and various policy measures have been adopted for promoting the livelihood status of tribal women. However, these programmes have not been successful to a significant extent. It is also revealed from the study that the simple low input intensive technologies in limited scale are quickly accepted by the tribes as they have relative advantages of compatibility with the tribal culture. Hence, there is a strong correlation between the acceptance of the development programmes and delivery of technology which leads to infer that there is a need to alter the development approach in order to achieve desired result.

REFERENCES

Awais, Mohammad, Tosib Alam and Mohd Asif (2009) 'Socio-economic Empowerment of Tribal Women: An Indian Perspective', *International Journal of Rural Studies*, 16 (1).

Blumberg, R.L. (1991) Income under Female versus Male Control: Hypotheses from a Theory of Gender Stratification and Data from the Third World. In R.L. Blumberg (Ed.), *Gender, Family and Economy: The Triple Overlap*. New Delhi: Sage Publications.

Bruce, J. and D. Dwyer (Eds) (1988) *A Home Divided: Women and Income in the Third World*. Stanford: Stanford University Press.

Census of India (2011) Registrar General and Census Commissioner. New Delhi: Government of India, Publications Division.

Chambers, Robert and G. Conway (1992) 'Sustainable Rural Livelihoods: Practical Concepts for the 21st Century', *IDS Discussion Paper 296*. Brighton: Institute for Development Studies.

Elson, D. and R. Pearson (1981) 'Nimble Fingers Make Cheap Workers: An Analysis of Women's Employment in Third World Export Manufacturing', *Feminist Review*, 7.

Evans, J.E. (1997) *Growth Prospects Study: Rapid Assessment of the Impact of Policy Changes on Rural Livelihoods in Malawi*. Washington, DC: World Bank.

Kanji, N. (1995) 'Gender, Poverty and Economic Adjustment in Harare, Zimbabwe', *Environment and Urbanization*, 7 (1).

Krantz, Lasse (2001) *The Sustainable Livelihood Approach to Poverty Reduction: An Introduction*. Stockholm: Division for Policy and Socio-Economic Analysis, Swedish International Development Cooperation Agency.

Menon-Sen, Kalyani (2001) *Gender, Governance and Feminisation of Poverty: A Country Perspective*. New York: UNDP.

Moser, C. (1996) *Confronting Crisis: A Comparative Study of Household Responses to Poverty and Vulnerability in Four Poor Urban Communities*. ESD Series, No. 8. Washington, DC: World Bank.

Narayan, D. (2000) *Voices of the Poor: Can Anyone Hear Us?* New York: Oxford University Press for World Bank.

Scheduled Castes and Scheduled Tribe Research and Training Institute (SCSTRTI) (2004) *Tribes of Orissa*. Odisha: Government of Odisha Press.

Society for Regional Research and Analysis (2010) *Migration of Tribal Women: Its Socio-economic Effects: An In-depth Study of Chhatisgarh, Jharkhand, M.P. and Orissa*. New Delhi: Government of India, Planning Commission.

UNDP (1999) Strengthening Natural Resource Management and Sustainable Livelihoods for Women in Tribal Orissa. Sub-programme Document under the Food Security Programme, New Delhi: UNDP.

9

Changing Scenario of Women Empowerment and Political Awareness among Gond Tribe of India

BHAWNA

We are on the threshold of the 21st century; India has witnessed a drastic change in women's empowerment in all the fields, e.g. economic, political and social. However Indian women have to go a long way in attaining gender equality and gender justice. India is one of the few countries where the constitution guarantees equal rights to Indian women. The provision of universal adult franchise has played an important role in the achievement of political equality and political participation of women. It is important to refer to the report of 'The World's Women' 2000 Trends and Statistics released by United Nation which says that India has improved its score in education, employment and per capita income of women but has not improved women's representation in politics, stressing the need to give women a place in decision-making for survival and progress of our democratic policies, as the participation of women is essential.

The present paper deals with the political awareness and participation among the Gond women through the reservation by 73rd Amendment as it leads the way to women's empowerment.

The empowerment is political, social, economic and cultural but with the attainment of political power through *Panchayati Raj* and participation in other elections, the women of Gond tribe will also be affected in their social, cultural and economic life. There are many studies on the role of Gond women in the cultural, social and economic field but political awareness among Gond tribal women is not included in most of the studies for example Grigson (1938), Singh (1976) and Singh (2011).

According to 2001 Census Report the total tribal population is 84.2 million and 8.2 per cent of the country's population. The population of tribes in Madhya Pradesh is 12.233 million constituting 20.27 per cent of the total population of Madhya Pradesh (60.385 million). The main tribal groups in Madhya Pradesh are Gond, Bhil, Baiga, Korku, Bhariya, Mariya, Saharia, Dhar, Jhabua Hatba and Kaul. Mandla district has more than 50 per cent of tribal population and maximum number is that of Gond tribe. The most famous women ruler and warrior who came from Gond tribe and fought against great Emperor Akbar and died in the battle field, was *Rani* Durgawati, but afterwards the Gond women did not get opportunities to become politically powerful. The tribes all over India are facing economic, social, religious and political backwardness. They are not benefitted from the different developmental schemes due to lack of education, poverty and lack of awareness of their constitutional provisions and rights. The Gond women have two-fold disadvantages – first being a woman and other is being a tribal. In both the conditions they are oppressed and exploited.

The present paper is concerned with the empowerment of Gond tribal women by the 73rd Constitution Amendment and political awareness. Women have a distinct role to play in the welfare and development of a democratic nation and Gond women cannot be deprived of those opportunities due to lack of participation and awareness.

There are about 700 tribal groups living in different parts of India. The tribal constitute 8.2 per cent of the Indian total population. It is surprising to mention that due to gender discrimination sex ratio in India is the lowest but female ratio among the tribes presents a better picture. The tribal women face poverty and hardships but they are not discriminated as other women in Indian society. But we can say that social and cultural life of tribal women is in the state of transition as they are coming in contact with outside world. In this paper I have tried to assess the level of empowerment through political awareness in present context as the tribal women have shown initiatives and courage to come forward and participate in decision-making process. Women's empowerment may be defined as transformation of the structure of subordination, including changes in the political, social and economic system. It gives more decision-making power, opportunities for participation and the control over the discriminatory practices.

According to Griffen (1987) the indicators of empowerment are:

1. Having control, organizing further control.
2. Having a say and being listened to.
3. Being able to define and create women's perspective.
4. Being able to influence social choices and decision affecting the whole society.
5. Being organized and respected as equal citizens and human beings with a positive contribution.

The empowerment of women through *Panchayati Raj* has the basic object to participate in development that leads to political, social and economic empowerment.

The greatest revolutionary change in the history of women's empowerment occurred when 73rd Constitutional Amendment Act was passed in 1993. The Act has provided one-third of the total seats reserved for women of which one third will be for the scheduled castes and schedule tribes. It is important to note that one third of the total posts of the office bearers at all level will be reserved for women in *Panchayati Raj*. In tribal areas one third of the reserved posts will belong to tribal women. In this study of tribal area, all *Panchayat* members are tribals and half of them are women instead of one third only. It encourages studying the effectiveness of women participation, awareness and aspirations for leadership.

Methodology and Objectives

The aim of the present paper is to study the changing scenario of Gond women's empowerment through political awareness.

For this purpose I had selected 100 Gond women of Bijadandi Block Mandla district (MP) where the Gond population is 84.64 per cent. This block has a population of 62,985 and out of this 53,310 are Gonds. I have also adopted case study method for extensive study and selected 10 Gond women for case study, 2 *Sarpanchs* (president of *gram panchayat*) and 8 other Gond women from the village.

Four villages have been selected from this block and from every village *Panchayat* 25 women were selected. Out of 25 women 5 women were the members of village *Panchayat*. I have studied in Tarwani, Magradha, Danwahi, Dungaria village. Women's participation, interest and responsibility are being studied as the members of *Panchayat* on one hand and on the other hand, remaining respondents as a part of general public.

All of the respondents are married and 90 per cent live in joint families. A large number of the respondents have never gone to school. Only 15 per cent have studied up to Junior High School, 12 per cent have studied up to Higher Secondary level and 8 per cent have a B.Sc., B.A. degree. Most of the respondents are found to be fighting against poverty. They either work on their own agricultural land or as labourers in farming, building construction, etc. while 2 per cent are working in the schools.

All the *Panchayats* are constituted by Gonds. The members are Gond males or Gond females.

The objectives of the study are as follows:

1. To determine the level of political participation in *Panchayat*, State Assembly and Parliament.
2. To determine the influence of personal, social and economic factors on political awareness.
3. To determine the level of women empowerment through political awareness and participation.
4. To examine the impact of 73rd Amendment of the Indian Constitution on the empowerment of women.

Findings

According to Mukhopadhyaya (1977) 'Political awareness provides the motive for understanding the political system thereby creating political participation'. While, Varshney (1988) states that 'Political awareness is the special feature of a society which gives a meaningful expression of the political attitudes and interests of the society. Political awareness can be understood by various related concepts like political participation, political interest and political responsibility'.

To determine the levels of awareness, following dimensions have been studied – political participation and political responsibility.

Political Participation

Political participation refers to the objective behaviour of an individual which is manifested in casting vote during election, contesting election, campaigning, taking part in agitations, attending public meetings and membership of political parties.

All the respondents enthusiastically go for voting even the women above 60 years of age go for voting, as they are motivated by their family members. The voters are more eager to vote for *Panchayat* election. About 95 per cent votes are cast in this election but they do not actively participate in Assembly or Parliament elections though in these elections also 76 per cent tribal women go for casting their votes. Out of 100 respondents I had taken 20 *Panchayat* members and other respondents were from general public. All the 15 members were motivated by the family or political party. Only 5 members contested election on their own choice. Only 12 per cent of the respondents wanted to contest in Assembly or Parliament but they said that Political parties do not give chance to women candidates. Only 20 per cent opted for campaigning and 5 per cent women went for campaigning to earn money. Others denied due to pressure of their work and family bindings. Around 12 per cent respondents are the members of different political parties. Bhartiya Janta Party (BJP) and Congress are prominent in this area. Nowadays they talk about Aam Admi Party (AAP) also but BJP is their first choice. They also know about Chutka movement. Tribal of Mandala district were organized against Chutka nuclear power plant proposed on the banks of Narmada river and the area falls in 'High damage risk' Seismic Zone. The strong mobilization forced the government to postpone the project and most of them also participated in that movement. About 90 per cent women believe that participation in politics will open the doors of development and empowerment of women. Around 100 per cent respondents are in favour of reservation in *Panchayati Raj* and they hope for 30 per cent reservation in Assembly and Parliament.

Political Responsibility

The women have a duty towards making India a better, stronger democracy which can be accomplished only through a process of socio-political transformation. A person feels concerned about the functioning of the political and social system specifically the functioning of *Panchayati Raj* after the 73rd Amendment Act. Three consequent terms (each term of five years) of *Panchayati Raj* have encouraged the womenfolk to understand the purpose and benefit of the system. They also feel that due to lack of education *Panchayat* members do not understand the functioning and government officers do not care for their advice and do not give them the opportunity to work independently. Only 5 per cent go to leaders to solve their problems. They also expressed their anger against the criminalization of political system and in this context they appreciated Anna Hazare and AAP because they are fighting against corruption.

The steady increase of women voters at each election shows that they feel a responsibility towards the nation.

Out of 20 *Panchayat* members only 2 members know about the 73rd Amendment Act's provisions, though they go to attend the meeting and they also tell their problems in the meeting.

The Gond women have aspiration for holding political positions. The women aspire to command respect in their community and they think that they will be away from household work and hard labour as they have to work in agricultural land. About 95 per cent *Panchayat* members want to continue their position as a member. Only 5 per cent do not want to contest *Panchayat* election due to family problems.

Case Studies

Case I

I had a long interview with Smt Prabha Tekam, *Sarpanch* of Dhanwahi village, Bijadandi Block, District Mandla. She is 28 years of age and she has passed B.A. As she is educated she knows about the political parties and she is the member of BJP. In her *Panchayat* the total members are 15 and women *Panchs* are 9. She is interested in politics and wants to contest election if given the chance by the party. She told that there are 40 *Panchayats* in Bijadandi Block and 22 *Sarpanch* are women. Only 18 males are *Sarpanch* and all the *Panchayats* are constituted with majority of Gond tribe. She is well versed with the problems of her area and she is eager to solve the problem of school, electricity, Primary Health Centre, roads, and toilets. She is also worried about unemployment of the villagers. She told me that most of the population is living in poverty. Women also work but they either labour on daily wages or work in farms. Some of them work as maids in different houses. She also insisted that they do not have girls school separately, they have to go to Jabalpur for higher education. The facilities of uniform and mid-day-meal are provided by the government in schools. They also have the facility of oldage pension but due to ignorance they do not get the benefit. She told me that she is trying to arrange these benefits for the area.

She is dissatisfied with the government officials as they do not cooperate in implementing the developmental programmes.

She wants to continue her position as she wants to work for the development of her village. She gets full cooperation from her husband, son and other members of the family. She lives in joint family and their occupation is agriculture having land of 3 acres. She feels responsible and committed towards her voters.

Case II

Munnibai Dhurve is the *Sarpanch* of Tarwani *gram panchayat*, Bijadandi Block, District Mandla. She is 44 and educated up to primary level. She wanted to study further but her parents did not allow her to go to the existing co-educational school. She has regrets of being deprived of education and so she is demanding that the local representatives of assembly start a school only for girls. She is also worried about the water problems. She wants to have a community hall for cultural programmes because she herself used to take part in their traditional dances. She told during the interview that women have to work hard as labourers as they do not have other options for earning money. Moreover, they do not have proper medical facilities. The Village Health Centre is usually closed due to absence of the doctor who rarely comes as he belongs to city. She said that though she regularly attends the meetings she cannot understand procedure of the meeting and her husband or her son go with her. There are 8 women *Panch* in her *Panchayat* but they are also less educated and not able to work for the development. She does not understand the agenda of the meeting but is eager to do developmental work and to solve the problems of the area. If government officers take proper care of the projects, the picture will be different. There are so many beneficiary schemes for the tribal which are to be implemented through *Sarpanch* and this can be successful only when *Sarpanch* is educated and understands the system.

For the purpose of case study I interviewed 8 other women who are not members of *Panchayats*. Only one woman, who was educated up to high school, knew about 73rd Amendment Act but she did not know about the provisions of the Act. Other 7 women knew only that there is reservation and women can be *Panch* but they had the opinion that the reservation is for rich class who have lot of land. When asked about contesting the election, 4 rejected the idea saying 'who will earn money' and 'the family will not like it'. When asked, a BJP worker also told that it is very difficult for them to select a woman candidate as they do not come out of their shell; they complained that women do not talk with them and sometimes they have to discuss all political matters with the male members of the family. Generally women also accused the *Sarpanch* and other members of swindling money from the schemes. Corruption has opened its wings in tribal area and most of the work is done through the male members and there are examples of accepting the bribes also. The women non-members also accepted that *Sarpanch* is doing work for the upliftment of the people. All the women are in favour of reservation and accept that if women join politics, they can do better work than the man.

Political Awareness

The success of democracy depends upon the political awareness of its citizens. Political awareness and activities of citizens are measures of democratic nature of the government. After the implementation of *Panchayati Raj* even in tribal areas the consciousness of the political participation and responsibility has increased among women. Voting ratio has increased more than 90 per cent. Votes are cast by the women. It shows their awareness of voting rights. The members of *Panchayat* told they contested the election reluctantly due to the pressure of family members but now they are interested even for the coming elections. They take interest in knowing the results of election. They are also aware that their lack of education is the main cause of their backwardness. For awareness, two factors are important and demand a new conceptual approach. The first is the extraordinary social and political transformation due to 73rd Amendment Act and second factor is the critical revision of the role of women in society and worldwide demand for gender equality and gender justice. These two factors opened the path of social and political awareness. Many organizations are working in tribal area for the awareness of women. Apart from political parties like Congress and BJP, Gondwana Gantantra Party, Matdata Jagaruk Sangh, Adim Jati Seva Sahkarita Sangh and other NGOs are working among the tribal people.

Conclusion and Recommendations

The basic objective of this study was to find out the level of political awareness among tribal women and its impact on the empowerment of tribal women. The subject is important on account of the need of the present society. In India we need the creation of an egalitarian social order which can ensure involvement and participation of the women in the process of country's development. In a democratic country women are expected to be the part of political system by their participation in elections, decision-making process, trying to influence the political system for solving their problems, attending public meetings and campaigning, etc.

For the purpose of the study three dimensions of awareness have been studied, political participation, political interest and political responsibility.

The study indicates the increasing level of awareness as the women are empowered through political participation. There is a steady increase in the percentage of casting votes. It is found that lack of education cannot restrict their interest in voting. It is also noted that age group from 25 to 35 is more interested in attending rallies and listening to speeches of political leaders. Due to poverty every family does not have a TV but they watch it in neighbour's house.

All the members of the *Panchayat* go to attend the meeting whether they understand the proceedings or not, they usually go with their husbands or sons. They desperately expressed the need for education as it would be helpful for work in political field. They are also aware of the problems faced by the villagers but unable to solve actively due to ignorance. On the whole we can say that the government has given the weapon of power in their hands but not the ability to use it. We require long-term scheme of educating the women to make their struggle successful. Political parties have also neglected their task of politically educating and mobilizing the Gond tribe.

The empowerment of tribal women from grass-roots level is the power given by the 73rd Amendment Act. It is evident that for the first time they have started to take interest in politics and their aspirations are high as some of them want to contest assembly and parliament election also. This political empowerment has led to social and economic development. It is also true that tribal women are passing through a transitional stage as they have been given the opportunity to participate in decision-making process but at the same time the lack of education and poverty push them back. It was indicated at the time of study that although they are aware of the opportunity and they are interested in coming forward, they need the support of family members, government officers, political parties, NGOs to motivate them to make themselves suitable to grab the opportunity.

To sum up, the tribal women are empowered through political awareness. They have started coming out of the shell of ignorance and acknowledging their potential as future tribal leaders. They are aware of the challenges and the need to emerge as empowered women.

From the findings of the study it is suggested that the tribal women should be provided with education at least primary education be compulsorily given to them. Government should open separate girls' high schools and colleges for them. This is important for understanding the policies, schemes and their own rights and responsibilities. I personally feel that some educational qualification should be compulsory in *Panchayati Raj* for proper functioning of the development programmes. The same should be considered for assembly and parliament's members.

My study indicates that there is a strong need of training programmes to make them aware of their responsibilities. They should be provided with the knowledge regarding the Act as it is observed in the study that they are not aware of the provisions of *Panchayati Raj* Act. Ministry of Tribal Welfare should take strong measurements to organize training camps for building confidence through knowledge and preparing them for planning for the development. NGOs should also come forward and organize camps including the members of different blocks and districts to exchange the views, and they will be aware of the working of the others also. The government officers should also be invited in these camps for encouragement and creating favourable atmosphere.

Most of the members of *Panchayati Raj* admitted that their husbands or sons go for the meeting. To build confidence, district authorities should ban them or discourage them to come for the meeting. It will enable the women members to have their own identity.

The study concludes that tribal women have started to open their wings and are aware of the challenges in the society. They know that they have to come out of their shell to participate in politics and share power. They will have to work twice as hard as their male counterparts in order to be recognized and make their presence felt.

REFERENCES

Griffen Vanessa (1987) *Women, Development and Empowerment*. Naboutini, Fiji: Pacific Women's Workshop, 23–26 March.

Grigson, W.G. (1938) *The Muria Gonds of Bastar*. London: Oxford University Press.

Mukhopadhyaya, A.K. (1977) *Political Sociology*. Calcutta: K.P. Bagchi & Co.

Singh, Brijesh Kumar (2011) *Gond Janjati mein Sanskritik Parivartan*. Varanasi: Bharati Prakashan.

Singh, Indrajeet (1976) *The Gondwana and their Gonds*. Bombay: Popular Publications.

United Nations (2000) *World's Women: Trends and Statistics*. Geneva: United Nations.

Varshney, Uma (1988) *Education for Political Socialization*. Faizabad: Unpublished Ph.D. thesis submitted to Avadh University.

10

Narratives of Himalayan Annies

'In My Next Life I Want To Be Reborn A Man'

SWATI AKSHAY SACHDEVA AND WINNIE BOTHE

Although Buddhism is often envisioned as a gender egalitarian religion, the cannon of Buddhism sends a mixed message. Moreover, gender relations have come to take on different meanings as Buddhism adjusted itself into the different societies in which it took hold. In tantric Buddhism[1] we specifically find how it philosophically took on more gender-neutral connotations (Josh 1967), although later stories explain women's religious degradation (Shaw 1994). In practice, however, tantric Buddhism has evolved into patriarchy where women take on a subdued religious role. Although this is well researched in the context of Tibet (Tucci 1970; Shambhala 2002), little is written on Buddhism and gender relations in the Himalayan states which are highly influenced by tantric Buddhism.

A review of the literature on Himalayan annies (women monks) of Sikkim and Bhutan reveals that there is a vacuum of research on the role of annies in the monastic culture and their position in the monastic hierarchy. In this paper we address how processes of traditionalizing Buddhism affects gender stigmatization within the monastic world in the Himalayan region in the periphery of Tibet. We concretely look into how religious narratives construct, promote and institutionalize particular roles for women in their spiritual lives.

The analysis was conducted on the basis of 50 qualitative interviews carried out in Sikkim in 2013 at the Chorten monastery, which is also referred to as a Bhutanese monastery because it has monks, annies and devotees visiting from Bhutan. The other monastery surveyed was the Rumtek monastery which was an all annie monastery, having annies from different parts of the Eastern Himalayas. A narrative approach is used for inquiry because it provides an effective way to undertake the systematic study of personal experiences of the respondents. By using this approach we were able to link events, perceptions and experiences and helped fill spaces in our research.

Historical Significance of Buddhism in Constructing Gender Relations

Religion has always influenced the position and identity of women in a society. Women are often regarded the harbingers and supporters of religion and faith. This was certainly the case with Buddhism at its beginning where women came to enjoy more equality and respect, than ever accorded to them. Before looking at the Buddhist literary sources and attitudes expressed toward women, we need to briefly consider the social context within which Buddhism arose and developed. Hinduism was not only known for oppression by its caste system, but also its treatment of women. Dharmasiri (1997: 138–172, 150) describes the culture at the time of the Buddha as one 'where the woman was by definition inferior to man and where woman was strictly stated to be the obedient servant and devotee of the husband'. In the meantime rapid urbanization of the eastern Gangetic valley and the emergence of a new sense of self-consciousness and individuality, especially among individuals who were marginalized, resulted in a widespread acceptance of Buddhism in society because Buddhism professed equality (Josh 1967: 368). Although women's activities were confined principally to domestic and social spheres, their religious position also began to improve. Buddhism provided a new opening for women to take on a religious role as the Buddha gave *dhamma* to both men and women equally as is reflected in the study of canonical literature, the *Jataka* books and *Milindapanho*. Moreover, he opened the religious spaces to female religious practitioners, although the question of whether he accorded these an egalitarian status remains contested (Sponberg 1992).

Mahayana literature displays a gradual evolution of a positive concept of women in terms of their wisdom and practice. Most significantly, it advocated the idea of a *Bodhisattva* figure that embodies the highest state of wisdom and compassion in which all sexual and social discrimination ceases to exist.[2] In this early Buddhist philosophy women's chance of achieving spiritual emancipation is equal to that of the men.

However, this positive and egalitarian image of women changed in later Buddhist history. In later Buddhist texts they are portrayed as jealous, ignorant, passionate and deceitful (Paul 1981). Buddhism inherited a view of women whereby if they are not represented as mothers then they are portrayed as either lustful temptresses or as evil incarnates.

Even Mahayana literature, although propounding an egalitarian view, does not unanimously uphold the equal status of women and they are often relegated to a secondary status. To be consistent with the Mahayanist egalitarian view towards all sentient beings, the motif of sex transformation was introduced into these *sutras*. If a woman's virtue, merit and wisdom are extraordinary, she may, through a sex change, become a *Bodhisattva* or a Buddha in her present or future life. Transformation of gender symbolizes a transition from the imperfect condition of a human being represented by the female body to the mental perfection of a *Bodhisattva* and Buddha represented by the male body.

Material for the account of the alms women (women monks) is found in the *Vinaya Pitaka* and the *Suttapitaka*.[3] However, even in earlier Buddhist texts like *Larger Sukhavativyuha sutra*[4] and *Smaller Sukhavativyuha*[5] we find an anti-feminine attitude which ranks female practitioners lower than male practitioners, an attribute it shares with other institutionalized religions. He specified that all nuns be subject to the authority of monks by the 'eight heavy precepts' *(lciba'ichosbrgyad, garudharma).* The first and most important of these eight rules dictates that a nun who has been ordained a hundred years must bow down to a monk ordained for only a day.

Although there is available literature which highlights the role of women and gender in Buddhist societies, they have not explored in depth the extraordinarily rich source of material available and the questions they raise. Many scholars (Gross 1993; Barnes 1994; Kajiyama 1982) have sought a narrow scope in analysing women's social and symbolic roles in Mahayana Buddhism. They have studied significant social shifts in the status of women's in different Buddhist traditions, like the question of women's attainment of Buddhahood, the shifting roles of women in contemporary Buddhist societies, including recent initiatives such as the move to reinstate full ordination for nuns. Historically speaking, Buddhist studies over a period of time have tended to focus more on men than their women counterparts, which has created a lopsided androcentric view of Buddhism. The primacy of text over other sources of knowledge has further accentuated the marginalization of role of women in Buddhism. Rather than rejecting religion for its inherent patriarchal notions, a feminist dialogue between members of Buddhist communities across the globe puts forward a new agenda pointing at the need to reinterpret the religious texts and systems in a way that is both coherent and consistent with traditional values as well as feminist notions of gender equality.

Women's Position in Vajrayana Buddhism

Vajrayana Buddhism was established in Tibet in the 8th century when *Úântarakita* (Great Buddhist Master of the Mahayana school was abbot of the Buddhist university of Nalanda) was brought to Tibet from India at the request of the Dharma King *Trisong Detsen*, sometime before 767 BC. He established the basis of what later came to be known as the *Nyingma* School.[6] As a Tantric master Padmasambhava's contribution can be credited with making Vajrayana a part of Tibetan Buddhism and from there it entered into Sikkim and Bhutan. In its origin Tantric Buddhism presents a gender egalitarian vision of women, because it theoretically resolves the distinction between the male and female, and ascribes to women an equal opportunity for receiving enlightenment as men. Padmasambhava advised *Yeshe Tsogyal* that far from being a hindrance to enlightenment, as was generally accepted, a woman's body is an asset. The basis for realizing enlightenment is a human body. In original Vajrayana philosophy, the female is symbolic of wisdom, while the male is symbolic of compassion, somewhat opposite of the way the sexes are viewed in the West. Women are considered to be superior practitioners to men as they are said to have a greater capacity for wisdom. The union of the male and female principles, compassion and wisdom, is known as *bodhicitta* (Wilson 1992; Allione 2000).

According to Campbell (2002) prior to Buddhism in these two countries the Bon religion existed which had a strong matriarchal component. It is also widely argued, that pre-Buddhist society in Sikkim and Bhutan held important matriarchal elements, which held female goddesses and deities as central objects of animistic practice, as testified by archaeological excavations. As Buddhism was introduced into Tibet it amalgamated existing local animistic practices, gods and goddesses. The feminine elements of the existing religion would have therefore fitted well with tantric philosophy that dissolved the binaries between the male and the female.

In Tantric Buddhism there are several examples of feminine embodiment, e.g. Tara is worshipped as an example of a female Buddha. Additionally there are female messenger of wisdom called *dakini*. The Tibetan word for *dakini* is *khandro* which indicates that these ethereal bodies are 'sky goers'.The *dakinis* are the most important elements of the enlightened feminine in Vajrayana. Additionally, *dakinis* are a female embodiment of enlightened energy and part of a tantric practice called the 'Three Roots'.[7] Women thus play a vital role in the practice of Vajrayana Buddhism and are essential to the attainment of the ultimate goal of enlightenment, placing the women at par with the men.

Here the importance of women begins to unfold. It implies that women should be treated justly because they are the essence of the goddesses and female Buddha that preceded them. By disrespecting a woman, you are disrespecting the goddess or Buddha that she embodies. This is a rather strong statement, because disrespecting a Buddha is truly offensive. The treatment of women became even more important to the male practitioner when the consequences of disrespect were laid out. These consequences may seem very severe, but it only goes to show how important it was that women be respected in Tantric Buddhism.

Later, however, Vajrayana Buddhism slowly evolved into a patriarchal religion. The move towards patriarchy within Vajrayana Buddhism remains under research. We suggest it may well be associated with the state building efforts of SangtenGambo, who unified Tibet and institutionalized Buddhism as a state religion in the 6th century. A theory is that in order to suppress the female aspects of religion and society, the female demonesses had to be subdued by the male Buddhist practitioners, in order to introduce a religious patriarchy. Most famously, SangtenGambo[8] had to nail down a demoness with temples in order for Buddhism to take hold in Tibet, and with it a patriarchal approach to religion. If this theory holds true, Buddhism, however, only managed to suppress the female aspects of the 'big religion' whereas such practices continue to survive in the 'small religion',[9] at least in the periphery of Tibet, Bhutan and Sikkim (Crins 2004: 588; Balikci 2008: 145).

In the following section we will uncover how Tantric Buddhism, despite gynocentric root bears androcentric flowers (Gutschow 2004), by looking into the philosophy and practice in two Buddhist monasteries in Sikkim. It, however, lies outside the scope of this paper to reflect upon the differences between these monasteries and the causes for these.

Gendering Monasticism: Hierarchy and Space

Gender hierarchies within Buddhism have a broader cultural impact upon the social attitudes of women (Puntarigvivat 2001). Traditional religious stories, images, and ideals reflect misogynist views in society but are also likely to reinforce these. This tends to result in the devaluation of women and their sexuality. Nonetheless, in a social context, Buddhist women have enjoyed more prestige and freedom in the Tibetan periphery of Bhutan and Sikkim than in either China or India, and probably also even more so than in Tibet itself.

In this section we will illuminate how contemporary Nyingmapa Buddhism seems more influenced by misogamist Indian texts than by the original wisdom of tantric masters, in particular GuroPad Rinpoche.[10]

What we came across in our fieldwork was that annies defined their religious identity on the basis of a comparison between ordinary women and themselves in the role as religious practitioners. They narrated how they were in better control of their mind after joining the monastic life. A Bhutanese annie found herself better placed in the monastic system than ordinary women:

R: First, the basic difference is based on our ability to control mind, annies have a better ability to control than ordinary women. Secondly, annies are away from five bad behavioural aspects (desire, anger, ego, jealousy and ignorance) whereas ordinary women are inclined towards it. Thirdly, Lord Buddha himself has said that, those who wear his sacred dresses and follow codes and conducts are considered superior than ordinary being (Anni Loday Wangmo, Age 33 years, interviewed on January 2014, Chorten, Deorali).

However another annie shared a different view on being a women:

R: I feel being a woman is a sin. We are like a dustbin. Buddha has called us that.

I: But Buddha regarded men and women as equal, why would he call women a dustbin?

R: He wanted to warn his disciples that is the reason he said this.

I: And you accept this?

R: (nods head)

I: Why do you think you are a 'dustbin', have you experienced anything which makes you feel that way?

R: I am a women. I have to obey (Annie Tshewang Dema, Age 25 years, Chorten, Deorali)

We investigated her story, whether it was descriptive or normative, whether it described the tendencies on the part of a particular individual or the group because of gender stereotyping. Another annie contested the 'dustbin' story, and said it was a misconstruction of Buddhism, whilst she tried to explain the unexplored meaning and interpretation behind it:

I: Did Buddha call women a dustbin?

R: This is always interpreted in a wrong way and no one has tried to clarify it. In fact the Buddha was trying to scold monks indirectly who were mostly attracted towards women. There were no nuns during that period so in order to divert the mindset of men from worldly desire towards the spiritual world, he had said '*Why you get attracted to such body, who's beauty is associated with dressing*' (Ani Loday Wangmo, Age 33 years, interviewed on January 2014, Chorten, Deorali)

The annie also shared another narrative to illuminate how women are viewed as religiously inferior. In this narrative a sixty-year-old lady had seduced a young monk (*Galong*) at high level in the monastery. According to their codes the *Galongs* are not supposed to have physical relation and thus his purity was at stake. The moral of the story was that women were regarded as inferior because they have more sexual desires. We frequently encountered such stories in the Chorten monastery. By contrast, we did not come across such degrading narratives of women in the Rumtek monastery. In this section we will explore the relationship between Buddhist text and contemporary gender narratives and practice which we found in the monasteries.

Monastic Ranks

In the monastic system ranks are determined by knowledge and ways that are followed. This classification of position is sketched in the *Sutrayana*, where monks and nuns are ranked accordingly. The first stage is known as *Gatshel* for men and *Gatshelma* for women and both should strictly follow ten vows.[11]

If they are able to follow ten vows then they are eligible to advance to the next position, called *Galong* for men and *Galongma* for women. To be *Galong* they need to follow two hundred fifty (250) vows and for getting initiated to a *Galongma* there are three hundred and sixty four (364) vows to be followed. According to the Khempo (Dorjee Thinley, 39) of Chorten monastery, these vows are written in the *Dulwa*. *Dulwa* outlines how a woman needs to conduct herself in front of a *Galong*. The Buddha said the monks are not supposed to disclose what is in the *Dulwa* until and unless they acquire that position.

As such, the rule that places monks above nuns in the monastic hierarchy is said to have its origin from the Buddha himself. Yet, its validity comes from centuries of repeated subordination as much as from the Vinaya or canonical monastic discipline where this is stated. Although the Buddha admitted that women can gain enlightenment just as men can, he only accepted women into his monastic order on one condition. He specified that all nuns be subject to the authority of monks by the 'eight heavy precepts' (*lciba'ichosbrgyad, garudharma*).This interpretation of the view of the Buddha was continually reproduced through monastic practice in the Chorten monastery as one of the annies' accounts:

I: Is there a strict monastic seating order?

R: Yes, there is a difference in sitting position of the annies, we are supposed to stay behind or in lower position compared to monks. It's a sign of respect because they have acquired more wisdom than us...they are men (Anikuenzang Choden, Age 56 years, interviewed on January 2014, Chorten, Deorali).

The gender hierarchy was also observed in the practice of reading and memorizing certain texts. It was rooted in a specific interpretation of core texts of Tantric Buddhism. This practice equally prevented women from learning religious texts as is described in a novel of a nun's story *The Circle of Karma: A Novel* (Kotti 2005). The *Dulwa* was one such text which the annies were prohibited from reading. The *Dulwa* constructed a negative image for the annies. In the words of a Bhutanese annie from the Chorten monastery:

I: What is the *Dulwa*? Why do you think women are not supposed to read the *Dulwa*?

R: *Dulwa* is a book based on ethics of body and speech; it is read by *Galongs* only. The reason why women are deprived of reading this book is based on an old story. Previously, women were also capable of being *Galongma* along with *Galongs*, but it got stopped from the reign of *Galongma* Pelma, who was a reincarnation of Lord Buddha. During that phase she didn't find apt women to whom she could impart all the wisdom

> which she had, and she died without finding a female reincarnation. Ever since, women's lineage has been cut off from reading the *Dulwa*, though some wished to study but due to lack of female teachers on this specific field they are unable to do so (Ani Tshewang Dema, Age 44 years, Chorten).

Nonetheless, other annies at the monastery informed us that it was possible to read the *Dulwa* if they reached the position of *Galongma*. The Khempo reiterated this view. He informed us that the *Dulwa* comprises of 'thirteen volumes'. It is not, that women in principal are not supposed to read the *Dulwa* but they are only allowed under one condition that they have to attain the position of *Galongma* taking three hundred and sixty four (364) vows. To guide them they need senior *Galongma* along with a *Galong*, but the problem is that the lineage of *Galongma* no longer exists, because at the time there were no women who were wise enough to follow such vows. Thus, women are only eligible to be *Gatshelma* (the lowest level) but not *Galongma*, and it is thus both taboo for both *Gatshelma* and *Gatshel* to read *Dulwa* and annies never have the opportunity of advancing beyond the lowest level. According to his opinion there is hardly any probability in contemporary context that women might attain such high position, because in one way or the other their path to the highest levels in the monastic order is obstructed. This kind of explanation produced discursive boundaries between the annies and the monks. When we inquired at the Rumtek Monastery about the *Dulwa*, they said they can read it. But when asked what it contained, they were unable to apprise us.

Reincarnation

While it is clear that in Buddhist tradition both men and women are subject of miseries of *Samsara*, women are in some text seen to suffer because of their bodies. According to Paul (1981: 6):

> Symbolically, women represented the profane world, *Samsara*. Perhaps more detrimentally women were potential obstacles in actual life to man's spiritual growth. In spite of the tantric vision of women as the locus of wisdom, the patriarchal impetuous of Buddhism seemed to penetrate the monasteries

> with the vision of women as having less intelligence, excessive attachment and uncontrollable desire. But more puzzling is that their religious role has come to be associated with misogynist ideas of religious impurity, because of their menstruation cycle and role in childbirth.

These views have tangible effect severely undermining the ability of monastic institutions to sustain them. Despite the monastic androgyny which is associated with renunciation of family life and traditional makers of gender like the hair, they continue to be re-sexed and characterized as suffering from the negative corporeality of being women. The women are viewed as impure because of their menstrual cycle.

R: Women are impure because, they can't control their tongue; girls have more knowledge to cheat others and have more sexual desire. Because of these reasons they are considered as impure.

I: Even men cannot control their tongue, so they are also impure?

R: We have menstruation which makes us impure (bad smell). During whole period in actual we are not supposed to do sacred tasks but tend to do those because of lack of alternatives (Ani Kezang Yuden, Age 67 years, Chorten, Deorali).

How this view of women as impure entered Tantric Buddhism is a mystery, given the initial equality ascribed to men and women in religion. A plausible explanation well may be an amalgamation between Buddhism and Hinduism, but it remains an unexplored ground. On the contrary, the annie at the Rumtek Monastery did not resonate a similar sentiment. In the words of an annie, they had entered the monastic world for a place of equality rather than inequality. Could this be explained by the fact that they were not contesting for space with the monks at the monastery?

I: If you were in a monastery where there are monks, do you think it will still be the same. Would you be allowed the same freedom you have now?

R: We meet them very briefly, so I cannot comment much.

I: Do you bow down to them?

R: Yes, I do, but that is out of respect and choice. But, we live separately, we have freedom. If we stay together then there is risk of impurity. So, in order to avoid this it is good we have different institutions.

I: What do you mean by impurity?

R: In 'our' monastery, we do everything during our periods, but in the 'big' monastery we are not supposed to. I have heard they are very particular. In this environment we can learn instruments without feeling shy of other opposite sex. We don't feel any sort of awkwardness. So the learning process is very much flexible (Ani Karma Chazom, Age 25 years, Rumtek).

Karma is the driving mechanism of the basic Buddhist theory of transmigration that, importantly, posits a particular relationship between mind/consciousness and the body upon which all Buddhist liberation are based. Mind and body are interconnected but the body acts a temporal for mind consciousness that moves from life after life within a gradation of six possible forms of existence, from human beings to God. A consciousness achieves rebirth in a better or worse form depending on the *karma* that has been accumulated in the form of merits and demerits. In Buddhist thought the body is essential, since it is the only chance in the cycle of rebirths to choose, it is the only route out of this endless trouble and suffering but this is polluting as well. The body seems to contain a natural orientation towards attachment and desire. Thus, the most liberating path advocates that one should transcend the body and see it as something defiling (Makley 2005: 268–269). Women's body were more closely associated with sexuality requiring containment and regulation. According to this Buddhist philosophy, sex differences produce different mind body relations and results in basic proclivities that differentiate a man and a woman. Associated with the body the male have more merit from past lives (ibid.: 270). Such views were reiterated by the annies. In the view of one:

I: Are men and women different, are annies and lamas different?

R: Yes, men and women are different. Women are born women, because of their bad deeds in their previous life as compared to the men. Men have done good deeds so that they have attained the life of manhood.

I: Do you think, things will be different if you were a man?

R: Yes, because by being a man I will be able to spread the doctrine to the masses and help the needy (Annie Pema, Age 56 years, Deorali).

Importantly, the bias for the lower status of the female body was on the assumption that it was burdened with physiological suffering as menstruation and childbirth. It is thus seen more difficult for them to obtain enlightenment because their cycle makeș them psychologically unstable. This was reflected in the narrative of Ani Kezang Yuden, Age 67 years, Chorten monastery.

I: What does being Buddhist practitioner mean to you?

R: It is a noble profession, because I know the prime purpose of my life. I am fortunate to be born as human being. It is really a difficult task and on top of that to devote life by being a religious practitioner is an added blessing. But I am a woman … . I cannot attain the next level in the religious field. I want to be born a man and fulfil this unfulfilled dream and attain nirvana. It is also said that there is a prayer in Buddhism, especially for those who have conceived which states that, 'let the foetus be a male'. This is because males are considered superior than women.[12] We are seven lives behind men.

In Tibetan folklore, women are seven lifetimes behind men. Women must accumulate the merit of seven additional lifetimes before they can be reborn as men. The proverb persists despite a rather dubious logic and this remains an area to be investigated. According to her the very nature of suffering is explicitly associated with the female body. The assumption of close relationship between women and suffering is long standing in Buddhism. Early Buddhist literature presents a list of unique situation of women's suffering; the 'Samyuta Nikaya' names five of these – (1) Leaving blood after marriage, (2)

Menstruation, (3) Pregnancy, (4) Giving birth, (5) Waiting for a man (Harris 1999: 54).[13] According to the respondents the female body is itself a *Samsara*. Women's bodies themselves are the negative system in this dualistic system of bondage and enlightenment. Male bodies are rewards for past merit or virtue; female bodies are to be reviled and rejected. The annies at the Rumtek Monastery did not agree in principal, some had heard about the seven lives concept and some had not. Similarly, this is why the funeral pyre of the women was eight layered as compared to the men that was seven layered, because they need the extra step to attain salvation (Mondal 1998/1999).

The Buddhist philosophy states that the role of women in Vajrayana Buddhism is equivalent to that of men. What our fieldwork signifies is that there was a difference how women practitioners look at themselves. Although they enter the monastic institutions regarding it a place of equality, their perception change after entering the monastic institution. We asked a lama at the monastery:

I: What does being a man mean to you?

R: Firstly, to be born as a human being is very difficult and on top of that to be born as a man is considered as a privilege.

I: So what does being a woman mean?

R: Women are born women due to their past karma. They have negative karma in their previous life. The variables for the negative karmas are '*mi gawachu*'[14, 15] or ten non-virtue deeds/actions to which women are prone to as compared to men. Women due to their fickle behaviour they tend to be victim of such sinful behaviours and because of which in their next life they tend to be born as women. So, I believe that if women in their present life check this loophole by devoting themselves to '*gawachu*',[16, 17] then in their next life they can be born as men (Lama Tashi Tobgay, Age 21 years, Chorten, Deorali).

Thus, we observed that Buddhist practices have perpetuated a consistent preference for monks over nuns. The ritual practices that produce merit and purity illustrate the sheer impossibility of transcending difference and rank. Doctrine may view duality as conventional and ultimately illusory; practice knows it to be real and necessary. While the female body signifies defilement and constraint, the male body suggests purity and potential. Ritual practices reinstate the subordination or subdual of female nature (Gutschow 2004).

Concluding Thought

His Holiness the Dalai Lama is the most important figure in Vajrayana Buddhism. Twenty or thirty years ago, a journalist from a French women's magazine had asked the Dalai Lama whether a Dalai Lama can be female incarnation in the future? And he had said 'yes' because the purpose of a reincarnation is to serve people through *dharma*, and, if the circumstances are such that a female form is more useful, then why not? However, Buddhist literature has produced a range of discourses about the relationship between sex and enlightenment. Tantric ideas of monastic androgyny thus look at a highly different form in the everyday life of the monastic world. In effect, it took on an opposite form of the ultimate ideal of transgressing gender ambiguity.

What we found was that patriarchal images of women's religious status strongly influenced the Chorten monastery, where the annies were relegated to an inferior role. By contrast, in the Rumtek monastery the annies were dedicated, successful practitioners and teachers of Buddhist wisdom and did not hold a negative image of themselves. According to Khempo the reason why women consider themselves as inferior is because there might be certain influence based on their cultures and traditions. Their mental perception depends upon how they are being socialized. This is advocated by society because there is no past *karma* philosophy nor is it mentioned in religious scripts. However, annies still continue to feel abandoned on the path of enlightenment.

R: There are no difficulties, but my prayer is that in the next life I should be born a man.

I: Why a man?

R: They get enlightenment faster (Ani Loday Wangmo, Age 33 years, interviewed on January 2014, Chorten, Deorali).

But in the words of another annie at the Rumtek monastery:

R: Even we can get enlightenment like the monk. I may be a women because of past life karma but in this life I can change it.

This difference in the influence of patriarchy may have its origin in two factors that were present in the two institutions under investigation. An obvious factor is sharing of the religious space between monks and annies in the Chorten monastery, whereas the Rumtek monastery was an all annie monastery. But perhaps a less obvious factor is the fact that the Chorten monastery was governed by a Bhutanese Rinpoche, and the monks, and annies predominantly came from Bhutan, whereas in the Rumtek monastery the practitioners mainly originated from Sikkim. This raises the puzzle as to whether the sharing of space affects the religious gender role of the annies and their position in the realm of Buddhism, or if this can better be ascribed to the nature of the state from which the religious practitioners originated. We thus find two possible entries into understanding the gendered competence. Firstly, the independence from male dominance in the annie monastery which may justify why gender stigmatization had less impact in the annie monastery, than in the monastery where men and women were sharing the space. Secondly, the difference in how the states were imagined may well account for the differences. Sikkim projected a 'modern' and multi-cultural image of itself, with religion referred to the margins of political life. Bhutan, by contrast, sought to project a 'traditional' and mono-cultural image of itself, in which Buddhism was seen as its very '*raison d'etre*'. Although, we will not be able to completely account for the difference, gender is a relative truth which must be ultimately abandoned as an illusion on the path to enlightenment. The traditionalized Buddhist practice of androgyny can open the possibility for a kind of resistance, but this indicates a need to rethink on a cultural logic for gender hierarchy.

NOTES

1. Tantric Buddhism is the third school of Buddhism that exists in the Himalayan nations of Tibet and Nepal. The word 'Tantric' means *Tantra*. The word '*tantra*' means books dealing with rituals, discipline, and meditation. Monks and priests in Tibet are known as lamas, so Tantric Buddhism is also called Lamaism. Tantric Buddhism first came to Tibet in the 7th century AD. It mixed together Indian Buddhism and Tibetan beliefs. This form of Buddhism is totally different from other forms of Buddhism. This type of Buddhism consists of worshipping by reciting prayers and sacred texts, along with chanting of hymns. Indian Buddhist tantric practices have been preserved in Tibetan Buddhism. A body of texts called the *Tantras* was written so that only initiates of a particular *guru* would be able to understand them.
2. The '*Vimalakirti Sutra*' and the '*Srimala Sutra*' belong to this category. In these two 'sutras' the position of the female reaches its highest peak. The doctrinal basis for this culmination lies in the Mahayana doctrines of '*sunyata*' (emptiness), '*Tathagatagarbha*', non-duality, etc. Instead of attempting to identify maleness with Bodhisattva hood and Buddhahood, the sutras in this category claim that notions of duality – either male or female, subject or object, etc. – are merely mental attachments contradicting the teaching of emptiness.
3. The Vinaya comprises of the rules and regulations for monastic discipline. It consists of two sections, the Bikkhunivibhaga and the Bikkhunikhadhaka, both of which deal with the code of conduct that the Bhikkhunis and female probationers should observe. These hold a great deal of gender equality with the belief that women may also attain enlightenment. The Suttapitaka, for instance, deals with the verses narrated by those nuns who had attained vision of nirvana or arahantship (Horner 1982).
4. The thirty-fourth vow of the '*Larger Sukhavativyuha-sutra*' states 'O Bhagavat, if, after I have obtained Bodhi, women in immeasurable, innumerable, inconceivable, immense Buddha countries on all sides after having heard my name, should allow carelessness to arise, should not turn their thoughts toward Bodhi, should, when they are free from birth, not despise their female nature, and if they being born again, should assume a second female nature, then may I not obtain the highest perfect knowledge'.

5. This declares that there are no women in the Pure Land.
6. The Nyingmapa, a Red Hat sect of Tibetan Buddhism, incorporates mysticism and local deities shared by the pre-Buddhist Bon religion, which has shamanic elements. The group particularly believes in hidden terma treasures. The Nyingma tradition actually comprises several distinct lineages that all trace their origins to the Indian master *Padmasambhava*
7. Dakinis also represent the Three Roots as they may manifest as a guru, a yidam or a protector.
8. The first ruler to unite Tibet was Songtsen-Gampo. Srong-btsan sgam-po (617–649 C.E.).
9. Small religion is the non-organized religion.
10. Padmasambhava was an 8th century master of Buddhist *tantra* who is credited with bringing *Vajrayana* to Tibet and Bhutan. He is revered today as one of the great patriarchs of *Tibetan Buddhism* and the founder of the Nyinmapa school. In Tibetan iconography he is the embodiment of the *dharmakaya*. He is sometimes called 'Guru Rinpoche', or precious guru. He was brought to Tibet during the reign of the Emperor Trisong Detsen (742–797). He is associated with the building of the first Buddhist monastery in Tibet, Samye Gompa.
11. The Gatshelma implies that women are not supposed to have sex, steal, kill, lie, touch gold and silver, have dinner, wear jewelry, apply perfume, sing or sleep on a king bed.
12. It's a prayer which is found in the book called *Dukarcheydu*.
13. There is a Pali version of a 'five obstructions story' extant in the Chinese *Bahudhatuka Sutta* of the *Majjhima-nikaya*: 'One of the qualities of a wise person is that he knows that a female cannot become ruler of the world of humans and gods .... He knows that it is not reasonable for a woman to become an arhat or truly enlightened one. He knows that it is reasonable for a man to become an arhat of truly enlightened one. He knows that it is not reasonable for a woman to become a Cakravartin king, Indra, Mara or a Brahma' (Nagata 2002: 282).
14. Ten non-virtue deeds which hinder individual's quest for spirituality or acts as a barrier to pursue religious activity. As compared to men women are prone to these ten bad/sinful behaviours.
15. Ten non-virtue actions are:
    i. Killing any living being
    ii. Stealing anything of value

   iii. Sexual misconduct
   iv. Lying
   v. Divisive talk
   vi. Harsh talk
   vii. Idle talk
   viii. Carving/Converting
   ix. Ill-will
   x. Wrong view
16. Ten virtuous deeds which will lead any individual to attain nirvana or eternal bliss.
17. Ten virtue actions are:
   i. Not to take a life
   ii. Not to take what is not given
   iii. Avoid sexual misconduct
   iv. Not to deceive
   v. Avoid slander of others
   vi. Avoid harsh words
   vii. Avoid empty speech
   viii. Avoid greedy thoughts
   ix. Not to be malicious
   x. Avoid the wrong view

REFERENCES

Allione, T. (2000) *Women of Wisdom*. Ithaca, New York: Snow Lion Publications.

Balikci, A. (2008) *Lamas, Shamans and Ancestors: Village Religion in Sikkim*. Vol. 17, Leiden: Brill Tibetan Studies Library.

Barnes, N.J. (1987) Buddhism. In Arvind Sharma (Ed.), *Women in World Religions*. Albany: State University of New York Press.

Bell, C. (1992) *Ritual Theory, Ritual Practice*. New York: Oxford University Press.

Brown, J.S. (2002) *Dakini's Warm Breath: The Feminine Principle in Tibetan Buddhism*. Boston: Shambhala.

Campbell, J. (2002). *Traveller in Space*. London: Continuum.

Changchub, G. and G. Nyingpo (1999) *Lady of the Lotus-Born: The Life and Enlightenment of Yeshe Tsogyal*. Padmakara Translation Group, Boston: Shambhala.

Crins, R. (2004) Religion and Gender Values in a Changing World. In K. Uraand Kinga and S. Thimphu (Eds), *The Spider and the Piglet: Proceedings of the First International Seminar on Bhutan Studies*. Thimpu: Bhutan Centre for Bhutan Studies.

Dharmasiri, G. (1997) Buddhism as the Greatest Ally of Feminism. In K.L. Dhammajoti et al. (Eds), *Recent Researches in Buddhist Studies: Essays in Honour of Professor Y. Karundasa*. Colombo: Y. Karundasa Felicitation Committee.

Gross, R.M. (1993) *Buddhism After Patriarchy: Feminist History, Analysis, and Reconstruction of Buddhism*. Albany: State University of New York Press.

Gutschow, K. (2004) *Being a Buddhist Nun: The Struggle for Enlightenment in the Himalayas*. Cambridge: Harvard University Press.

Gyatso, J. and H. Havnevik (2005) Introduction. In C. Bell (Ed.), *Women in Tibet: Past and Present*. New Delhi: Motilal Banarsidass.

Harris, E.J. (1999) The Female in Buddhism. In K.L. Tsomo (Ed.), *Buddhist Women Across Cultures: Realisations*. New York: State University of New York Press.

Horner, I.B. (1982) *Women in Early Buddhist Literature* (A Lecture to the All-Ceylon Buddhist Women's Association Colombo, Sri Lanka, 18 January 1961, Buddhist Publication Society in the Himalayas). London: Harvard University Press.

Josh, L.M. (1967) *Studies in Buddhist Culture of India*. Delhi: Motilal Banarsidass.

Kajiyama, Y. (1982) 'Women in Buddhism', *Eastern Buddhist*, 15 (2).

Kotti, S.R. (2005) *The Circle of Karma: A Voice from Bhutan, India*. New Delhi: Zubaan-Penguin Books.

Kunsang, E.P. (1993) *The Lotus-Born: The Life Story of Padmasambhava*. Recorded by Yeshe Tsogyal. Bostan: Shambhala.

Makley, C.E. (2005) The Body of a Nun: Nunhood and Gender in Contemporary Amdo. In J. Gyato and H. Havneik (Eds), *Women in Tibet*. New York: Columbia University Press.

Mondal, R.S. (1998/1999) 'Status of Bhutia Women of Darjeeling Himalayas: A Profile', *Himalayan Miscellany*, 12 and 13.

Nagata, M. (2002) Transitions in Attitudes to Women in the Buddhist Canon: The Three Obligations, the Five Obstructions, and the Eight Rules of Reverence. Trans. by P. Watt. In B. Ruch (Ed.), *Engendering Faith: Women and Buddhism in Premodern Japan*. Michigan: University of Michigan Press.

Paul, D. (1981) 'Buddhist Attitudes towards Women's Bodies', *Buddhist-Christian Studies*, 1.

Peach, L.J. (2000) 'Human Rights, Religion and (Sexual) Slavery', *Annual of the Society of Christian Ethics*, 20.

Puntarigvivat, T. (2001) A Thai Buddhist Perspective. In J.C. Raines and D.C. Maguire (Eds), *What Men Owe to Women: Men's Voices from World Religions*. New York: State University of New York Press.

Rowlands, J. (1998) A Word of the Times, but What Does it Mean? Empowerment in the Discourse and Practice of Development. In H. Afshar (Ed.), *Women and Empowerment: Illustrations of the Third World*. Basingstoke: Macmillan.

Shaw, M. (1994) *Passionate Enlightenment: Women in Tantric Buddhism*. Princeton, NJ: Princeton University Press.

Sponberg, A. (1992) Attitudes toward Women and the Feminine in Early Buddhism. In J.I. Cabezon (Ed.), *Buddhism, Sexuality, and Gender*. Albany: State University of New York Press.

Tucci, G. (1970) *The Religions of Tibet*. Berkeley: University of California Press.

Walters, J. (1994) *A Voice from the Silence: The Buddha's Mother's Story*. Cambridge: Cambridge University Press.

Wilson, L. (1996) *Charming Cadavers: Horrific Figurations of the Feminine in Indian Buddhist Hagiographic Literature*. Chicago: University of Chicago Press.

Wilson, M. (1992) *In Praise of Tara: Songs to the Saviouress*. Boston: Wisdom Publications.

11

Understanding Learning Disability

A Study of Maternal Empowerment in Ghaziabad (India)

RICHA CHOWDHARY

The purpose of this paper is to describe how 'impairment and disability' are encountered within a north Indian context, and what implications this has for the provision of disability services. It is impossible to provide a comprehensive analysis, since India is not only a country but a sub continent, with a population beyond one billion people. Therefore, the social, political and economic complexion of India is extremely diverse, particularly in terms of its class and caste composition and the diversity of religious faiths found within that country. This paper is based upon research, the majority of the material collected for this paper was collected during the study conducted by Society for Human Empowerment and Ecological Protection (SHWEP), a non-governmental organization (NGO) but it also draws upon the limited secondary sources that were available. The study describes and critiques the theoretical understandings of disability and the philosophy and operational practice of Community-Based Rehabilitation (CBR) and awareness level of females living in Ghaziabad locality, before considering how each of these can mutually enhance and develop the other. This paper will focus upon the experience of disablement within a north Indian context. SHWEP interacted with families having a child with Learning Disability (LD).

Nature and Extent of Disability

The objective of this section is to explore what it is like to experience and what are the implications of having an impairment in a social context in India. As an integral part of the study disabled children's parents were specifically asked about the manner in which they perceived their children's disabilities and the social attitudes they encountered within their local communities in relation to their impairments and disabilities. They were also asked questions about what problems and difficulties they encountered as a result of their impairments, as well as what their needs and aspirations were for the future. The vast majority of those interviewed were clients in receipt of services provided by the NGOs that agreed to participate in this study. It therefore could be said that the disabled people interviewed were untypical of the majority of disabled people who live in Ghaziabad, since the majority are not in receipt of any services whatsoever. Where respondents (Both, family and children) had a severe cognitive impairment, their parents spoke on their behalf. The analysis presented below does not claim to be representative of the manner in which disabled people are generally perceived throughout India as a whole, nor indeed solely within the Delhi/National Capital Region (NCR). The result presented only provides a snapshot of the attitudes encountered by those who took part in this study. However, the conclusions and inferences that are drawn from the study concur with the analysis of other small scale anthropological studies that have previously been undertaken regarding disability in north India.

In total, approximately 30 families of disabled people participated in interviews conducted for this research, one-thirds of them were men. However, it was invariably the case that the quality of interviews was greater in group settings than when disabled child mothers were interviewed individually. The range of impairments encountered by the disabled who participated in this study were very diverse. They included those who were totally slow learners, those with partial or extremely affected Intelligence Quotient (IQ), cerebral palsy, etc.

Community Attitudes towards Disabled People

Disabled children's families who were interviewed encountered a multiplicity of reactions and attitudes from members of the local communities. It was stated during the course of several interviews that many community members showed a complete lack of understanding and awareness of the problems and issues encountered by disabled people. For example, the disabled are treated like objects of pity. However, these disabled people were generally invited to social functions but invariably felt uncomfortable in attending.

Beliefs regarding the causes of disability varied between urban and rural areas. Within the former, beliefs regarding the etiology of impairments are more likely to equate with western understandings that take account of explanations derived from medical science. However, within rural areas, the causes of disability and resulting impairments are frequently seen in a religious context. Within the traditional Hindu religion, disability is sometimes perceived to be the result of *karma*, whereby impairments and the resultant disability is considered to be the result of either the sins committed by one's parents, or alternatively, the consequence of the sins that one has committed during a previous life. Hence, disability is perceived as a recompense or retribution for past misdemeanors. The understanding given to the presence or absence of impairments certainly has a moral dimension to it. Mr Pankenel (an independent disability consultant), was of the opinion that there was widespread ignorance regarding the causes of disability throughout India. One participant who was interviewed, stated the following – '*Whether people in the community have met disabled people or not, they still believe that disability is a result of karma or sins of the past. Disabled people and their families are despised. People are afraid to come in contact with disabled people. They think that disability is contagious. Some people in the community tell people to avoid disabled people because they might also attract the bad luck of the disabled person and the family*' (Group Interview with Disabled People).

Children with disabilities are likely to experience further isolation and exclusion from their local communities because some parents feel a great deal of shame, remorse and guilt because of their child's physical or cognitive condition. In such situations, there is a tendency of parents to attempt to shun away their children. I have been told of instances where children have literally been locked up in their houses in an attempt to hide them, thus, avoiding their public disgrace. During the study I was told of an instance where one very high ranking civil servant had an 18-years-old son with cerebral palsy. The father, because of his high social position was fearful of the public disgrace that would be inflicted on his family because of his disabled son, had actually incarcerated his son in a bamboo cage for the first 15 years of his life. This action indicates that social standing within society is all important within India, even to the extent of being detrimental to members of one's immediate family. However, there is evidence to suggest that this instance of abuse is not an isolated case but is commonly encountered by disabled people, particularly in the case of women (International Disability Foundation 1999).

Relationship between Poverty, Employment and Disablement in India

The impact of poverty and disability is also reflected in the data presented herein. Father Cultinha, from the Divine Light Trust, was of the opinion that disabled people from low status families are often perceived as an economic burden. Endemic poverty often characterizes low status families, which was further exasperated by the presence of a disabled child who is unable to provide an economic contribution to the household. Disabled children from high status families sometimes find being accepted by their families difficult, due to the fear of bringing social disgrace and embarrassment upon them. Also, the prevalence of having a disabled sibling within the family is likely to be greater within low status households, since those living on very low incomes are susceptible to malnutrition, a lack of sanitation, poor housing and so forth. Erb and Harriss-White (1996: 82) stated:

> Disability is determined according to whether or not an individual is able to work. Conditions such as pain, alcoholism and swelling, to name a few, are conditions which are not disabling in a western setting, but are disabling in an agricultural and rural economy dependent upon sustained manual labour.

The Gender Dimension to Disability

A further important factor, that is potentially of major importance when discussing the provision of disability services in a society such as India is the social position of female and female child with disabilities. From the analysis of both primary and secondary sources, it is readily apparent that disabled women, both in India and internationally, have a relatively lower status than their male counterparts and are thereby less likely to receive and benefit from the provision of rehabilitation services. It is interesting to note that small scale studies have showed a men: women gender imbalance in the prevalence rate of mental disabilities in the order of 2:1 (Subramanya 1983 cf. Prabhu 1993). Thus, as in the case with physical and sensory disabilities, it does indeed seem that men are more likely to be impaired than women. The issue of the inter-relationship between gender and disability is increasingly becoming a topic of interest and discussion within the field of disability studies. Boylan (1991: 3) stated:

> In developing countries, a woman's status is considered to be subjugated and dependent. Families in rural areas do not send their able-bodied girls to school once they attain puberty. Even within the sisterhood of women with disabilities, there are those whose handicaps provoke even further discrimination particularly the mentally retarded and the blind.

What is Learning Disability (LD)?

Classifications and definitions of LD date back to the beginning of the last century and are inherently tied to older notions of organically based behaviour disorders minimal brain injury, and minimal brain dysfunction as well as the notion of dyslexia. In the 1960s, researchers, clinicians, and parents began to recognize that when all children with behaviour and achievement problems were lumped together, the group was heterogeneous and amorphous, which ruled out concepts such as minimal brain dysfunction. Instead, there was a branching off of children whose primary problem was behavioural (now called Attention-Deficit/Hyperactivity Disorder [ADHD]) and children whose primary problem was achievement. Although the term dyslexia had been available since the beginning of the century and was popularized by the work of Samuel Orton, not all children with achievement problems had reading difficulties. Thus, in the early 1960s, a group of researchers, clinicians and parents used the term learning disabilities.

LD Cannot be Defined Solely by Exclusion

The essence of the LD construct is the idea that low achievement is 'unexpected', representing people who struggle to learn, to read, write or do math despite the absence of conditions that typically interfere with success. This is why early attempts to identify LD focused on the exclusion of known causes of low achievement. Unfortunately, this approach to the measurement of unexpected underachievement has not been successful because the resultant LD subgroup is still heterogeneous. Since unexpected underachievement is a construct that cannot be directly observed, much like IQ or ADHD, it should not be defined independently of how it is measured. When the approach to measurement is to simply eliminate known causes, the definition is empty and imprecise.

LD Must be Defined with Inclusionary Characteristics

Since it is not sufficient to define LD solely by excluding known causes of low achievement, we need inclusionary criteria that specify the presence of LD. An immediately apparent inclusionary criterion is low achievement. Indeed, it must be established that the person with LD has low academic achievement in some area. However, other exclusionary criteria co-occur with LD, which makes it difficult to assess their causal significance. For example, these are behavioural and emotional difficulties (e.g. ADHD, anxiety, depression) often present in conjunction with LD and may be a consequence of the adjustment difficulties associated with poor school performance. Other definitional exclusions have not held up well in objective research, such as the assumption that economically disadvantaged children or children with minority language proficiency cannot have LD.

Inclusionary Markers of Unexpected Underachievement

In the past 20 years, several additional inclusionary characteristics have been proposed as markers of unexpected underachievement. These include IQ-achievement discrepancy, as epitomized in the 1977 federal regulatory definition; discrepancies among different domains of cognitive functions (i.e. unexpected underachievement signaled by a pattern of strengths and weaknesses apparent when 'psychological processes' are assessed) and instructional response.

This model is reflected in Individual with Disability in Education Act (IDEA) 2004 as a chronological age discrepancy model, i.e. 'a pattern of strengths and weaknesses in performance, achievement, or both, relative to age'. Low-achievement models have a considerable evidence base that reflects the extent to which these models are used in research and generate predictable differences in a variety of dimensions. For example, in groups of children who read above and below the 20th percentile, assessments of cognitive skills, intervention response and neurobiological correlates (Grigorenko 2005; Schlaggar and McCandliss 2007) can reliably differentiate achievement subgroups.

Aptitude-Achievement Discrepancy

Although early studies suggested that a significant discrepancy between IQ and achievement demarcated unexpected underachievement (Rutter and Yule 1975), this hypothesis has not held up. In the most extensive studies involving children with LD, comparisons of groups defined as IQ-discrepant and non-discrepant poor readers do not show meaningful differences in prognosis, cognitive skills related to the reading process (e.g. phonological awareness) or instructional response once definitional variability is accounted for in the models (Stuebing et al. 2002). Unlike Rutter and Yule (1975), these studies generally exclude children with mental retardation and brain injuries, which accounted for the 'poor reader' group in that study. There are also major psychometric problems attributable to the small measurement error of IQ and achievement tests, the fact that math and reading scores are normally distributed in the population and other factors that make most testing models based on a single assessment unreliable for identifying LD.

Cognitive Skills

Another proposed marker of unexpected underachievement is uneven development of cognitive skills such as phonological awareness, rapid naming, and working memory. To some extent, this position is based on the IDEA statutory definition, which associates LD with 'a disorder of psychological processes'. A person might be identified as having LD if they showed low achievement and strengths in some aspects of cognitive processing.

This model is not encouraged by IDEA 2004 and no provisions are made for it in the regulations. In fact, IDEA has never made routine assessment of cognitive processing part of the regulations because of the absence of evidence that these assessments provide unique information for identification and treatment planning, despite the routine use of these forms of testing in assessments of LD. First, such assessments should not be used to identify children as having LD in the absence of evidence of low achievement. Thus, a child who has poor performance on a phonological awareness test, but average reading, is likely a false positive error (Torgesen 2002).

Altogether, once achievement is assessed, what value do assessments of cognitive processes add to what we know about the person, given that achievement and cognitive processes are correlated? Individuals with basic reading problems (e.g. difficulties with word recognition) reliably display problems on tests of phonological processing. The assessment of phonological processing abilities therefore adds little to treatment planning or identification that is not indicated by assessing word reading skills. Phonological processing does relate to word reading, and because it does predict LD in this domain, it should be assessed in children who have not had formal reading instruction. Finally, cognitive assessment is justified by some because of the belief that the presence of a cognitive deficit affirms that the achievement deficit is biological in origin. To continue the word reading analogy, even economically disadvantaged children with word reading problems respond positively to explicit reading instruction, show phonological processing problems, and even fail to activate the temporal-parietal areas of the left hemisphere in a functional neuro imaging study.

Instructional Response

Most definitions indicate that LD should not be identified in the absence of adequate instruction. A major problem identified repeatedly in recent consensus reports is that children are identified and placed in special education under the LD category when core instructional programmes are not adequate for many children. Instructional response can only be reliably measured by assessing growth in academic skills in relation to instruction, which includes assessments of the quality of the instruction (Stecker, Fuchs and Fuchs 2005). Thus, inadequate response to quality instruction can be used to identify individuals for whom instruction is adequate, but who are hard to teach (Fuchs and Fuchs 1998; Vaughn and Fuchs 2003). People are identified as LD when they demonstrate low achievement and intractability to appropriate instruction.

A Hybrid Model for LD Identification

One component of IDEA 2004 that is often puzzling is a provision that allows states and districts to use other alternative research-based procedures for determining whether a child has a specific learning disability. Study suggests that all states should adopt an alternative model.

1. Student demonstrates low achievement.
2. There is insufficient response to effective, research-based interventions. A systematic plan for assessing change in performance must be established prior to intervention.
3. Exclusion factors such as mental retardation, sensory deficits, serious emotional disturbance, language minority children (where lack of proficiency in English accounts for measured achievement deficits) and lack of opportunity to learn should be considered.

Identifying children with LD, a clinic outside of school or in research, requires the presence of low achievement and in adequate response to instruction as inclusionary criteria. This is true whether the overarching identification model stems from an RTI process or from some type of psychometric model.

In addition, low achievement and poor treatment response may be due to other disabilities such as a sensory problem, mental retardation or another pervasive disturbance of cognition. Contextual factors that interfere with achievement, such as limited language proficiency (based on an assessment of achievement in local and the minority language whenever possible), co-occurring behavioural problems and economic disadvantage should be considered. However, it is important to emphasize that the chief consideration should be intractability in instructional response because objective criteria for distinguishing unexpected low achievement in children with behavioural difficulties and economic disadvantage are not presently available.

Early Definitions

The definition of LD in federal statutes is widely acknowledged as vague and difficult to operationalize. Consider the opening sentence of the current statutory definition, which first appeared in 1968:

> The term specific learning disability means a disorder in one or more of the basic psychological processes involved in understanding or in using language, spoken or written, which may manifest itself in an imperfect ability to listen, speak, read, write, spell or to do mathematical calculations... (US Department of Education 1968).

In 1977, a single inclusionary criterion was added for each of the areas in which LD could occur:

> ... a severe discrepancy between achievement and intellectual ability in one or more of the areas: (1) oral expression; (2) listening comprehension; (3) written expression; (4) basic reading skill; (5) reading comprehension; (6) mathematics calculation; or (7) mathematic reasoning (US Department of Education 1977).

The seven areas in which underachievement may occur were changed in IDEA 2004 to eight domains, essentially by adding reading fluency and changing mathematics reasoning to mathematics problem solving. The IDEA 2004 definition allows school districts to choose identification models that represent alternative inclusionary criteria, including a model based on Response To Intervention (RTI): 'The child does not make sufficient progress to meet age or State-approved, grade-level standards in one or more of the [eight areas of achievement]...when using a process based on the child's response to scientific, research-based intervention'. Finally, in perhaps the most significant change, IDEA 2004 provides an additional inclusionary criterion that must be assessed regardless of the identification model employed.

RTI is an Inclusionary Criterion under IDEA 2004

One way to understand the changes in the 1977 and IDEA 2004 regulations is to consider the nature of the inclusionary criteria. Although all versions of the IDEA legislation have required multiple assessments and multiple criteria for identification of any child with a disability, the 1977 regulations clearly led many districts to emphasize identification models based on IQ achievement discrepancy, focusing on a set of psychometric test scores that were often used as a gate keeping mechanism for LD eligibility determination. Thus, the 1977 regulations used a single inclusionary criterion (IQ discrepancy) and required consideration of the exclusionary criteria. Although subsequent reauthorizations of IDEA added as an exclusion the expectation that low achievement was not due to inadequate instruction, the IDEA 2004 statute and the regulations require assessment of this criterion, so that it represents an inclusion criterion.

First Reactions as Mother of LD Child

Grief is one of the most common reactions parents have when they find out that their child has a disability. Before having a child with disability, parents might have had dreams about how their child might be or how they imagined they'd be as a parent. Shock, anger, sadness, fear and resentment are only a few of the feelings that parents can have when they learn that a child has disability or illness. They might also wonder 'Why me?' or 'What have I done to deserve this?'.

Stress

Coping with the additional amount of physical and emotional care is a challenge. Children with disability can need regular medical attention, time in hospital or regular therapy, in addition to extra care at home. Depending on the severity of the disability, the child might need constant supervision. This pressure and the sense of isolation that can accompany high levels of care can place a lot of emotional stress on parents, and might affect the parental relationship or the family's ability to cope financially. Because of these stresses, emotional disturbances such as anxiety or depression are more common than usual among parents of children with disability.

Coping

Families of a child with disability cope better when they're supported by their partner, other family members or community services. Having two parents to contribute to care, finances and emotional support can make parenting easier. Parents who have a positive attitude and who look at the advantages they have over other parents also tend to cope in a more healthy way.

It was suggested to them – 'If you feel as though you can't cope, it can help to speak to a professional, such as a psychologist or counselor who will understand the stresses associated with your role'.

Methodology of Study

The purpose of this study is to describe the occupational concerns and goals of mothers who care for children with disabilities.

Retrospective data collected from 30 mothers of children with disabilities using the SHWEP and empowerment techniques for better occupational performance were analysed.

Six ways emerged (Techniques used to empower mothers for better rearing practices in these cases): (i) doing and being alone: taking care of my own health and well-being; (ii) doing and being with others: expanding my social life; (iii) improving my child's quality of life; (iv) household management: organizing time and resources; (v) balancing work, home and community responsibilities; and (vi) sharing the workload.

Results and Findings of the Study

Analysis ultimately yielded six ways (Techniques) that were able to circumscribe and describe the meanings associated with caring for a child with a disability. This section is taken at random and verbatim from the total data pool.

Way (Technique) I – Doing and Being Alone: Taking Care of My Own Health and Well-Being

One of the mother's goals, 'wear hair down more often', provides the general feeling of this theme: a desire to unwind and let down. The domain includes specific occupational goals to support personal health and well-being, including taking time to enjoy self-care rituals, exercise, recreation, relaxation and sleep. Examples of goals include: go to the bathroom by myself/take a shower on own schedule, have more time for me (to get a haircut, to eat lunch), jog/be more consistent with fitness program/workout on daily basis for 30 minutes, learn to relax and enjoy myself even when my regular responsibilities haven't been met, and get adequate amount of sleep on a more consistent basis with fewer interruptions. On a more internal level, this category also includes goals related to spiritual renewal, emotional processing, building self-esteem and feeling good. One of the mothers specifically wrote, 'have time alone once a week', and the goal 'time alone', was frequently cited.

Way (Technique) II – Doing and Being with Others: Expanding My Social Life

The second theme centres around making, maintaining and renewing relationships as well as keeping in touch, whether physically (visiting, traveling, getting together), by phone or by writing letters and e-mail. These occupational goals entail bringing together nuclear family, extended family and friends. Examples of goals include: 'going on picnics with family, spend more of my free time doing fun things with kids and spend time with other women like me'.

Way (Technique) III – Improving My Child's Quality of Life

The third theme could be summed up in the words of one mother: 'find strategies, find solutions, find a way'. The occupational goals in this category are directed at the work a mother does, including advocacy, to help her child to meet his or her potential. Verbs used by the mothers to describe this process include 'help, facilitate, develop, establish, structure, discipline and encourage'.

Way (Technique) IV – Household Management: Organizing Time and Resources

It involves tasks that comprise the daily routine. The 'to do' list for these mothers includes: cook, clean, weed out clothes in the closet, do laundry, fix and mend, iron, budget, pay bills, shop, run errands, get hair done, vacuum, landscape, mow, repaint, and redecorate. Mothers strive for efficiency in performance of chores through improved (time) management skills. A list of common verbs used in this category includes develop strategies, schedule, form routines, systematize, plan and organize.

Way (Technique) V – Balancing Work, Home and Community Responsibilities

The fifth theme focuses on getting out into the bigger world to advance professionally, improve the family's financial situation and contribute to society through volunteer and advocacy work. In pursuing desires and actions inherent to this category, some of the mothers' goals displayed explicit recognition that sustainable participation in work and community-related occupations was dependent on interweaving activities within the home/family routine.

Way (Technique) VI – Sharing the Workload

The sixth category relates to mothers' desires to relinquish responsibilities by having other persons assume them. Finding a trustworthy and reliable childcare helper was the top, oft repeated goal in this domain followed by a desire for husbands, significant others and children to meet more of their own needs independently and to assume more active roles in helping to maintain the household. Goals include: 'finding a dependable babysitter who has the skills and knowledge to meet son's needs, would like husband to find more flexible, understanding job, reach a compromise with spouse (each sharing responsibility), would like children to be more independent in self-care activities and being able to delegate without feeling like I have to be the one in control'.

Overarching Ways – Beyond Traditional Performance Areas: Overarching Temporal, Social and Emotional Contexts

Although the SHWEP organizes information around the performance areas of self-care, productivity and leisure, our desire was to look beyond this conventional triumvirate with the hope of gaining new insights into occupation and occupational performance, its affordances and constraints, and its meaning in the lives of mothers of children with disabilities.

Contextual elements that stood out as being particularly meaningful to the occupational performance of mothers of children with disabilities include the temporal, social and emotional.

Importance of Time

The mothers referred over and over to a desire to find time, make time, and to have more time. One participant stated, 'It's a powerful sense which states that there's never enough time'. Examples include: 'I have time to do housework without distractions, would like to spend less time in the park (going to therapy, grocery), find an optimal time to go grocery shopping by myself and time for myself to do things I enjoy doing'.

Parental time constraints may differ as a result of child-specific variables; some studies indicate a correlation between time costs, the degree of the child's disability and the presence of behavioural problems in the child.

Time considerations seem to have a considerable impact on quieter, more reflective occupations, which may be the first to go when 'push comes to shove' in the daily routine. Although the majority of goals identified by the women in this study could be classified as those that involve active doing, a substantial number, particularly within the domains of ways I and II, were oriented around time and space for just being alone or being with others. Being has been described as 'time to discover themselves, to think, to reflect and, to simply exist'. These goals encompassed time for 'dealing' with emotions, time for mental reflection and clarification and time for being together with others, including: dealing with anger and depression, time for solitude and peace, more time to reflect on future, private time with just my family doing something fun, spending own time with or without sacrificing my own time, being alone with younger son, go away for weekends with my friends, make time to socialize with friends and more time to play with children.

In addition to the scarcity of time experienced by mothers of children with special needs for doing and being, the quality of their time when engaged in occupations appears to be fragmented. The choppy, stop-and-go quality of their routines may prevent these women from realizing a satisfying rhythm, or tempo, during performance of occupations and preclude them from having optimal flow experiences. This may result from alternating back and forth between two or more activities when multitasking, and the need to frequently stop what they are doing in order to attend to their child's demands. This quality, as reflected in the mothers' goals, is characterized by interruption, disruption, distraction, and rushing. The goals express the mothers' tandem desire to do things at their own personally satisfying pace, as well as to separate occupations so that they may concentrate on one thing at a time: getting enough uninterrupted sleep, have time to do housework without distractions, getting children to therapy, doctor without rushing or stress, be able to shop for clothes in a relaxed manner, take a shower on own schedule, taking time to get ready (nice), have a good restful night's sleep and wake up when fresh, have a day each week to clean and work outside when everyone else is out of the house and doing housework while son is occupied (playing or sleeping).

The literature identifies various time-use strategies that have been used by mothers to different ends. Bateson (1996) coined the term 'enfolded activities' as a description of women's work that includes all that can be done while caring for a child. Although the strategy of enfolding occupation often results from multitasking and may lead to exhaustion, showed positive effects from the use of this strategy; she found that mothers of typically developing preschool aged children had fun when doing household chores that embedded play activities with their child. Building on the idea of enfolded activity, Segal (2000) identified the use of 'temporal unfolding' or doing only one thing at a time, by mothers of children with ADHD. She noted that mothers used this strategy to give full attention to their child in order to facilitate the child's success in reaching developmental goal. Outcomes from the use of strategies to enfold and unfold activities are varied and require more study to determine how they may be affected by complex personal and familial factors. Our data also reflects the use of additional strategies by mothers of children with disabilities to compensate for time constraints. One of these is a straight-forward attempt to stretch the wakeful hours of the day: 'get up earlier and be completely ready for my day before kids wake up.' Another strategy is to form organized and efficient schedules and routines: 'develop more organized system of filing, toy management, and establish daily household management routine/maintaining a morning routine'. It described how mothers of children with disabilities use routines and schedules to maintain a sense of control. Finally, some mothers interweave public and private work in order to support the family routine: 'need family-friendly position (individualized work plan), work as much as possible from home/finding a job (that will fit family's schedule) and balancing work and home responsibilities'.

Importance of Social Contact

Mothers of children with special needs also seem to be at high risk of social isolation. Multiple factors related to being the primary caregiver may deter participation in social activities for mothers of children with disabilities including volume of daily care giving activities, physical and emotional exhaustion, social stigma due to child's inappropriate behaviours in public places, and practical concerns related to transporting the child such as physical access and medical need. Four subgroups related to socialization and a desire to be in closer contact with others comprise this theme, (a) being together as a family, (b) spending time with kids or with husband, (c) staying in touch with extended family, and (d) making, communicating with and getting together with friends.

Dealing with Emotions

Both the interviewees and the member of SHEWP (who escorted researcher to the field) highlighted the prominence of painful emotions for these mothers.

A story was told by the member about a family with two daughters, the elder of whom had a disability and, at 7 years of age, had never been invited to celebrate a peer's birthday; her typically developing sister, at the same age, had a history of invitations to birthday parties. The mother who related this story talked about the feelings of anguish, disappointment and grief this brought for her. The mothers' occupational goals made reference to a variety of hassles and difficult emotions, including anger, depression, embarrassment, rejection, guilt, being overwhelmed, grief, fight-flight mode, stress, worry, exhaustion and ordeal.

Limitations of the Study

Limitations to this study include a sample composed of women in a predominantly middle and lower middle income bracket situated in Ghaziabad, UP, India. Use of retrospective data, although adequate for descriptive purposes, involves interpretation of textual artifacts removed from their contextual moorings by an objectifying researcher. The use of an inter subjective methodology would provide a richer understanding of the meaning of occupation in the lives of mothers of children with disabilities.

Conclusion (Implications for Practice)

Overarching patterns in the data suggested that the occupational performance of mothers of children with disabilities is constrained by time, overlaid by difficult emotions, and involves a desire for increased social contact. Qualitative analysis of data may provide insight into contextual factors that affect occupational performance as well as signaling point of entry for therapists to facilitate client centred occupational goals. A strong plea was made by mothers who participated in the member-check phase of this study for therapists to confront their own imperfections, to put energy into their own emotional and spiritual growth and to practice with heart. They expressed higher value and appreciation for therapists who touch their children, who look for the spirit behind the disability and who provide social support than for therapists who maintain an aloof stance as technical experts. The importance of therapists' social support for mothers of children with special needs has been documented in the literature.

In addition to providing social support, therapists need to maintain awareness of the power differential within the therapeutic relationship when working with these women and to put energy into creating a more equal playing field. Although mothers of children with disabilities are a diverse group, they are at high risk for social disenfranchisement and occupational marginalization, due to a variety of factors, including gender and loss of discretionary occupations that may lead to restricted participation in professional and community affairs. By enabling collaboration throughout all phases of the therapeutic process including during assessment, problem identification, goal setting, critique of treatment options, and determination of intervention efficacy therapists increase their clients' participation and socially empower them in the process. Doing this effectively in practice may be facilitated by the use of client-centred tools that support an enabling process.

REFERENCES

Bateson, M.C. (1996) Enfold Activity and the Concept of Occupation. In R. Zemke and F. Clark (Eds), *Occupational Science: The Evolving Discipline*. Philadelphia: F.A. Davis.

Boylan, E. (1991) *Women and Disability*. London: Zed Books.

Erb, S. and B. Harriss-White (1996) *Outcast from Social Welfare? Adult Disability and Development in Rural India*. Unpublished paper. Queen Elizabeth House, Oxford: University of Oxford.

Fuchs, L.S. and D. Fuchs (1998) *Treatment Validity: A Unifying Concept for Reconceptualising the Identification of Learning Disabilities*. UK: Emerald Group Publishing Limited.

Grigorenko, E.L. (2005) 'A Conservative Meta-analysis of Linkage and Linkage-association Studies of Developmental Dyslexia', *Scientific Studies of Reading*, 9 (3).

International Disability Foundation (1999) *The World Disability Report: Disability*. London: The Winchester Group.

Morris, J. (1991) *Pride Against Prejudice*. London: The Women Press.

Prabhu, G. (1993) 'Mental Handicap in India: A Situation Analysis', *Action Aid Disability News*, 4 (1).

Rutter, M. and W. Yule (1975) 'The Concept of Specific Reading Retardation', *Journal of Child Psychology and Psychiatry and Allied Discipline*, 16 (3).

Siegel, L.S. (1992) 'An Evaluation of the Regression Discrepancy Method for Identifying Children with Learning Disabilities', *Journal of Special Education*, 14.

Stecker, P.M., L.S. Fuchs and D. Fuchs (2005) 'Using Curriculum-based Measurement to Improve Student Achievement: Review of Research', *Psychology in the Schools*, 42 (8).

Stuebing, K.K. et al. (2002) 'Validity of IQ-discrepancy Classification of Reading Disabilities: A Meta-analysis', *American Educational Research Journal*, 39 (2).

Torgesen, J.K. (2002) Empirical and Theoretical Support for Direct Diagnosis of Learning Disabilities by Assessment of Intrinsic Processing Weaknesses. In R.B. Radley, L. Danielson and D. Hallahan (Eds), *Identification of Learning Disabilities: Research to Practice*. Mahwan, NJ: Lawrence Erlbaum.

U.S. Department of Education (2004) Individuals with Disabilities Education Improvement Act of 2004. Public Law 108–446.

Vaughn, S. and L.S. Fuchs (2003) 'Redefining Learning Disabilities as Inadequate Response to Instruction: The Promise and Potential Problems', *Learning Disabilities Research and Practice*, 18 (3).

Contributors

Saroj Arora is working as Senior Research Officer in the Centre for Rural Studies, Lal Bahadur Shastri National Academy of Administration, Mussoorie, Uttarakhand. She is a Ph.D. from Punjab University, Chandigarh. Her areas of interest are gender issues, land reforms, land administration, displacement and resettlement and rehabilitation, agriculture, contract farming, environment and natural resources, watershed management, agrarian structure, health, water and sanitation.

Bhawna is the Head of Department of Sociology, Mahila Maha Vidyalaya P.G. College, Kanpur. She has participated in various national and international conferences and seminars. She has published four books and more than a dozen of papers in reputed journals. She has also published various articles in leading newspapers and magazines. She has written self-learning materials for Madhya Pradesh Bhoj (open) University. Her areas of interests are violence against women, empowerment, political awareness among women, gender discrimination and tribal women. She is the member of different social organizations working for the welfare of women.

Winnie Bothe is a Post-Doctoral Fellow at Lund University. She completed her Ph.D. at Copenhagen University in 2011, with the title – 'Forming Local Citizens in Bhutan: The Traditionalization of Participation, Empowerment, Domination or Subjugation?'. She publishes on the topic of gender, citizenship, local governance and civilization in South Asia. Her present Post-Doc project is a comparative analysis on Bhutan and Sikkim, illuminating how different languages of the state constructs citizenship.

Zhang Chao is a Ph.D. candidate at School of Public Policy and Management in Tsinghua University, major in public administration. His research focuses on Civil Society and Governance, Public communication and NGO. Up to now, he has published six articles mainly related to social movements, contentious politics and social policies in the core journals.

Richa Chowdhary is an Associate Professor of Social Work at B.R.A. College, University of Delhi. She completed her undergraduate education from BHU, Varanasi, and Masters and Ph.D. in Social Work from Lucknow University. She is associated with a number of governmental and Non-Governmental organizations, is on the board of studies at a couple of Indian Universities, is on the board of assessment agencies for NGO rating in India, and acts as head examiner at several universities of India. Presently she is involved in various research projects with different levels of organizations, and is also guiding research students.

Debashis Debnath is an Associate Professor in the Indian Institute of Forest Management in Bhopal where he has been working since 1994. He obtained his first class Honours degree in Anthropology with National Merit Scholarship from Government of India, got first class Master of Science (M.Sc.) degree in Anthropology with the specialization in Socio-cultural Anthropology and was awarded the Ph.D. degree in 1992 from Calcutta University. He was awarded the very coveted Premchand Roychand Scholarship with the Mouat (Gold) medal by Calcutta University in 2000. He worked in the Anthropological Survey of India (Government of India) for more than 5 years. His area of research interests are indigenous knowledge system and livelihoods development, tribal development and development management, forest governance and climate change. He has published three books and many research papers and articles in peer-reviewed journals and edited books.

Yoko Fujikake was awarded a Doctorate Degree from Ochanomizu University, Japan and is currently professor at the Institute of Urban Innovation, Graduate School of Yokohama National University. She was a Japan Overseas Cooperation Volunteer (Paraguay); a technical cooperation expert (Paraguay, Peru, Honduras, Tunisia); a guest researcher at the Institute for International Cooperation (presently the JICA Research Institute) of the Japan International Cooperation Agency (JICA); and associate professor at the Graduate School of Tokyo Kasei Gakuin University, Japan. Specialties include Development Anthropology, Gender and Development, Paraguay Area studies and principal literary works include, 'Qualitative Evaluation: Evaluating People's Empowerment', *Japan Evaluation Society*, Vol. 8(2) 2008, and *International Handbook of Gender and Poverty: Concepts, Research, Policy* (with Edward Elgar) 2010. As a leading representative of the NGO – Mitai-Mitakunai Foundation, she is actively participating in projects promoting rural women's empowerment and the construction of schools for children in rural area of Paraguay.

Anu H. Gupta is an Assistant Professor at the Institute of Fashion Technology and Vocational Development, Panjab University, Chandigarh. She is Masters in Clothing and Textiles and has worked on training of artisans on skill and design development. Her research interests include traditional textiles, handicrafts, embroidery, surface enrichments and subjects related to apparel industry.

Dong Isbister is an Assistant Professor of Women's and Gender Studies in University of Wisconsin, Platteville, USA. She received her M.A. in the Department of English, Michigan State University in 2001, and her Ph.D. in the Department of Women's Studies, Ohio State University in 2009. Her research interests include History and Memory Studies, Identity Studies, Transnational Cultural and Literary

Studies, Transnational Feminism, Qualitative Research, Asian American Culture and Diaspora Studies. She has published more than 8 research papers in both academic journals and conference proceedings in her research areas.

Sameera Maiti is a Professor in the Department of Anthropology and Dean, School of Human Sciences, Sikkim University, India. Prior to this she had been working in the University of Lucknow from where she had also received her M.A. and Ph.D. degrees. Prof. Maiti was awarded two gold medals, for ranking first in M.A. Anthropology and for writing the best fieldwork-based thesis for her degree. She is a past recipient of the National Fellow in Arts (2003-04) by Ministry of Cultural Affairs, Government of India and is a National Associate at the Indian Institute of Advanced Studies, Shimla since 2010. She has been awarded the Charles Wallace Visiting Fellowship to Queens University, Belfast (2004-05) and the Commonwealth Academic Staff Fellow (2011-12) to Oxford University. She was also awarded the Raman Fellowship by MHRD and UGC India in 2014. She has successfully completed two major research projects funded by the University Grants Commission. She is an executive member of various Anthropological Associations and the Associate Editor of *The Eastern Anthropologist*. As a keen researcher, Maiti has published two books and several research papers in various international and national journals. Her research interests broadly lie in the study of Anthropology and Art, (including material cultures and performing arts); Gender issues; Developmental issues and their acceptance thereof by marginalized, rural, vulnerable and tribal communities; Studies on exclusion, deprivation and inclusion; Health and ethno-medicinal issues; and Demographic issues.

Shalina Mehta is a Professor of Cultural and Social Anthropology in the Department of Anthropology, Panjab University, Chandigarh. She has edited, co-edited and authored 7 books and has 70 research papers to her credit. Her research areas include gender studies, environment, intercommunity relations and HIV AIDS.

Swati Akshay Sachdeva is an Associate Professor with the Department of Sociology, at Sikkim University. She has worked on the Bhutia society of Sikkim and women's position in the social fabric of this society. She has various National and International publications to her credit and has also published two books. Her areas of specialization are Gender Studies, Political Sociology, Culture studies and Eastern Himalayas. She is currently working on a project in collaboration with Department of Microbiology, Sikkim University. She was a part of the research team for the Sikkim Human Development Report 2014 and contributed immensely to the chapter on Gender. She has extensively worked on the problem of suicide and drug abuse in the state of Sikkim. She is a motivational speaker and has organize workshops on counselling and personality development.

Chinmayee Satpathy is an ICSSR Postdoctoral Fellow in the NKC Centre for Development Studies, Bhubaneswar, Odisha. She was a recipient of UNESCO Fellowship in 2007-08 in the honour of former Prime Minister of Japan Mr Keizo Obuchi, and successfully accomplished her research study on Indo USA Intercultural Dialogue in the University of South Florida, Tampa, USA. Satpathy was awarded Doctorate Degree in Sociology from Utkal University, Vani Vihar, Odisha in 2006. She has a long experience in working for the development of poor women and children belonging to tribal communities in the remote rural and tribal areas of Odisha in collaboration with various Ministries of the Government of India such as Ministry of Tribal Affairs, Ministry of Youth Affairs and Sports, Ministry of Health and Family Welfare, NABARD and National Commission for Women. Her research papers and articles have been published in many reputed journals and books.

Prem Singh is an IAS of 2000 Batch from Manipur, Tripura Cadre. At present he is Deputy Director and Centre Director, Centre for Rural Studies, Lal Bahadur Shastri National Academy of Administration, Mussoorie, Uttarakhand. He did MBBS from JIPMER from Puducherry. He has also done Postgraduate Programme in Public Management and Policy

(PGP-PMP) from Indian Institute of Management, Ahmedabad. His areas of interest include land administration, applied economics of welfare state, and service delivery in social sector (health and education).

Wang Xiaoli is associated with China Institute for Rural Studies, School of Public Policy and Management, Tsinghua University, Beijing, China. She is a post-doctorate and her research focuses on rural women's rights. She is currently working with State Family Planning Commission's team on Gender Equality and Village Governance. On May 2013, her research paper was submitted to the central leadership, and received reply from the Vice Premier Liu Yandong, 'The ACWF should work in cooperation with the Ministry of Agriculture, Ministry of Civil Affairs, Ministry of Land and Resources, and the Office of Legislative Affairs, to resolve relevant issues properly.'

Xiang Yixiao is an Associate Professor of Tourism Management in the School of Management, Shandong University, China. She received both her B.A. and her M.A. in English language and literature from Shandong University, China, her Master's degree on hotel, tourism and leisure management from Esthua, University of Angers, France, and her Ph.D. from Faculty of Environmental Studies, University of Waterloo, Canada. She has been teaching courses on tourism planning and management including ecotourism, world heritage and tourism, introduction to tourism resource, advanced topics on international tourism development (either in English or bilingual). Her research interests are heritage tourism and community studies (particularly tourism and local communities, especially rural communities on and around world heritage sites in China), politics of tourism planning and management in China, and sustainability of tourism, resource and community. She has published more than 15 research papers in both academic journals and conference proceedings in her research areas.

Index